He Uttered "Soulmate"

A THENA C OLEMAN

This book is a work of non-fiction. Unless otherwise noted, the author and the publisher make no explicit guarantees as to the accuracy of the information contained in this book and in some cases, names of people and places have been altered to protect their privacy.

LifeRich Publishing is a registered trademark of The Reader's Digest Association, Inc.

LifeRich Publishing books may be ordered through booksellers or by contacting:

LifeRich Publishing
1663 Liberty Drive
Bloomington, IN 47403
www.liferichpublishing.com
1 (888) 238-8637

Because of the dynamic nature of the Internet, any web addresses or links contained in this book may have changed since publication and may no longer be valid. The views expressed in this work are solely those of the author and do not necessarily reflect the views of the publisher, and the publisher hereby disclaims any responsibility for them.

Any people depicted in stock imagery provided by Thinkstock are models, and such images are being used for illustrative purposes only. Certain stock imagery © Thinkstock.

ISBN: 978-1-4897-0938-7 (sc)
ISBN: 978-1-4897-0939-4 (hc)
ISBN: 978-1-4897-0937-0 (e)

Library of Congress Control Number: 2016913832

Print information available on the last page.

LifeRich Publishing rev. date: 04/27/2017

To my daughter, Esprit, who helps keep me on my toes. To Mom who I miss so much and was very blessed to have.

For Dad who showed us a good work ethic and provided for us with many blessings from above.

For my dear nieces and nephews.

In remembrance of my 5th grade teacher, Mr. Skinner who assigned 25 cursive book reports due in 10 days (I thank him) and …

For You

Blessed is the
influence of
one true, loving
human soul on another.
- George Eliot

Contents

Contents

Preface

As the Great I am made the heavens and the earth and rested on the 7th day so too there were 7 words so there are 7 chapters. This memoir is a recollection of events as they happened and is true. Some information was withheld, but it is important to note that God can and will put you right where you need to be so that you are even able to recognize those who are integral to what will turn out to be your testimony. Where people need to be protected or to avoid offense, I have altered names and/or did not mention in the memoir.

Before embarking on my trip to the Mid-South from VA in 1999, I conferred and prayed to the Lord that I was headed to the Mid-South. I asked that he would lead me and guide me. Although I was feeling sad and sorry about leaving "home", I had to. In 2003, I had a dream a famous actor had a heart attack. It turned out that it was a younger actor who was cast as the older actor's name who had suffered the then believed heart attack. It was a comedy involving three roommates, two women, (one blonde, one brunette and a sandy-haired guy and their zany neighbors. This show aired in 1976. A social worker/member of Fellowship Baptist Church said the (dream) was a premonition.

One day after having a palpable sense of the meaning of a word that I had never bothered to define, I felt that I needed to start keeping record of what I would later call My "Second Wind." After reading this memoir, I hope you can find your place in God's story and start your "Second wind."

Chapter 1

Tumultuous (2005)

I had seen the word a couple of times in a book or magazine article, but the use of the word did not lend a clue as to what it meant, but after being sick and tired of being sick and tired, I now knew what the word tumultuous meant because I was feeling it. I was feeling the word tumultuous that it described my relationship and what my relationship was beginning to feel like. Tumultuous is defined as stormy, turbulent, volatile, violent, and explosive. Anyone would feel this way and ask themselves "What am I doing?" if you found that having an intelligent discussion in the ride home from viewing Hustle and Flow, you tell your daughter that you feel the movie was about going after your dreams in life and Bellows Creek tells you to "Shut up, don't nobody want to hear that stuff." Then a few weeks later with the pan still sizzling, we got into it over a hill of beans in a hallway inside the hospital. I just stopped short of finishing what I was going to say and walked away. It was Fall so it was cool, but warm if you were doing some sort of physical activity, and I kept walking right out the door of the hospital, down the stairs and on down the street. My saying is "Have feet, will travel." I had gotten pretty far before he realized I was gone and here he comes riding up beside me, but I ignored him and kept walking.

Chapter 2

Fortitude

And guess what? The word fortitude popped in my head and Honey, let me tell you this is definitely one virtue I have oceans of. I was just so mad and sick of dealing with the crap that I almost made it all the way home, walking. I was sick and tired of being sick and tired, and after that my silence started......

I first noticed Tristan's personality. Each time I saw him, he was always kind, friendly and exuding with energy. It did not matter where his path took him. Tristan could talk to anyone with the same tone and interest, and he had a beautiful personality. I only saw Tristan once every two weeks, but I had seen him on and off plenty of times before. The times that I saw him walking past by himself he would always say, "My friend." I would be sitting in the department alone and he would come through my department, walk by and say, "My friend." He would say it while walking and looking straight ahead, almost in a daze it seemed. The funny thing about it and the reason why it caught my attention is that my Daddy used to say "Well, my friend how much will that be at those times we were at a gas station, the bakery store at Campostella in Chesapeake or H. Salt Fish and Chips the seafood place.

One day, I and a few of my co-workers were talking about the café's food. The food was not amazing. They said it was horrible and the workers did not know what they were doing. But at different parts of the conversation, Tristan and I gave the cafeteria workers the benefit of the doubt. Tristan put his right arm around my right shoulder like a buddy or pal. I did not think anything of it for a long time until I started to have feelings for Tristan. I pondered whether he was already taken and said to myself, "I don't know who she is, but she is a lucky girl."

A month went by, and I thought of him every day. I even said to one of the other girls, "We have to get you married, how about Tristan?" One of them said he seemed like a "bully" because he was too nice. Another said, "I do not know about him; he seems to keep his private life just that." One day while at work we were sharing with each other how many kids we had. One of my coworkers asked him how many kids he had. His reply was very low-toned, and subtle. I did not hear anything that would give a hint.

The weather had started to change just slightly, and one evening I left a note for him that said, "Lately, the nights are getting colder. I would like two cups of hot chocolate with you and some interesting conversation." And I signed it, "Your Secret Admirer." Admire means to regard with admiration, to marvel at, to like very much. I realized that there were over 100 women who worked in the facility, and I only saw him every two weeks. Other women had more access to him than me, but when I walked by with them, there is no jealousy, because I know I am a woman to be reckoned with, and probably even the younger ones can't hold a stick up to me in quality as far as being a woman. I am a woman who used to catch footballs with my brother and his friends.

I am a woman who checks my own oil and fluids in the car. I am a woman who can and will "pimp" like a guy (game face) when I feel a little nervous about my safety. About a month later, I was still thinking about Tristan and Fall changed into Winter.

I woke up on Christmas morning 2005 and even though my eyes were open, I could not see anything. It was totally dark and I could not see anything. I was rendered totally blind by the Holy Spirit. I lie in bed for a few seconds to make sure I was awake and not dreaming. I was not really scared, but was beginning to get a little concerned when I heard the Holy Spirit say, "Someone significant is going to die after Christmas." I got really afraid then because I thought that maybe that someone was me. I tried to contain my thoughts and wondered who the Holy Spirit was referring to. Was it going to be me? My father who is almost 90? Esprit, my daughter? I had to summon patience nonexistent at the time just as it was when my mother was in the hospital for 6 months, a year before she passed. Later that morning when the Sun finally rose, I went to the store. Later when I went to work I gave everyone a Holiday bag with chocolate candy. Tristan was on the phone at the time, so I hand signaled that one of the bags was his. It had a color picture of beautiful snowflakes all over. He mouthed, "Okay" and "Thank you!" The next day, December 26, I went to his office and asked him did he have a lot to buy for Christmas. He said, "Tons." I smiled shyly, put one hand in my jeans pocket and walked out the door.

Two weeks later, we passed one another by the Anthropology reading area, and I said, "I see you again." He replied, "I see you again." After watching him and liking what I saw, I began to like myself more, and I realized my own good qualities, and that "dang Skippy", I had something to offer any man that would respect me. I started to internalize the song, "This is forth every best in you" –Change because I felt to sweet, so refined and such the lovely lady. I could not think of any

more holidays with which to send a card except Valentine's Day which was up next, and I decided to tell Tristan who his Secret Admirer was. I purchased from the store a card, and a big business envelope to secure the Valentine's card with package tape.

I wrote, "I've been watching you go about your days. You have mettle.

You have a great personality and an energy that has caught my eye and you have shown me that you have good character just as I do. I feel I am worthy of a man like you (man of your status, not necessarily you). The note also revealed that I had a faint feeling that he had some little ones that he was trying to help grow into productive citizens, and that I did not want to step on anyone's toes if there was indeed a significant other, girlfriend, fiancé, partner or wife. Because he shined so bright for me, and to me but not because of me, I began to put things in perspective about my own life. I wanted to know everything there was to know about him. I wanted to know him both latitude and longitudinally meaning... What kind of movies he liked? What is his mother's name? What kind of stories has he read? Does he have any brothers or sisters? What are his fears? What made him decide to work in the facility? What is his father's name? How or why was he named Tristan? Did he play ball in school? What year did he graduate? What college did he go to? Was he born in Tennessee? How many children did Tristan have? Did he let his kids watch the "Ten Commandments"? Did he know Jesus as his personal savior? Were his parents still living? Was he an only child? How does he feel about current events? I wanted to know all there was to know about him.

I was still thinking about the someone significant who was going to pass away.

After receiving a Valentine's card and note, Tristan said, "I appreciate that!" but he said nothing else. A week later I called him. I was so nervous I had to write down what I wanted to say to him. He sounded happy to hear from me. I asked did I get him in trouble with the Valentine's card, but forgot that I told him to throw it away if need be. He said, "No." I also asked was there a phone number or email address that I could have to chat with him more, but Tristan said, "No, I'll have to talk with you here." I knew that he was busy, so I just said to have a good week. After I hung up the receiver, I said to myself, "I knew he had a girlfriend" but he said that he would talk with me here." I did not recall a ring on his finger, and if he was not married, he was fair game.

Chapter 3

Soulmate

I started thinking about Tristan every night. He is the man I have been looking for all of my life. One night as I lay in bed, and thought about Tristan, the Holy Spirit said, "Soulmate." I said to myself, Soulmate? I wonder what that is? Of course I could not sleep then so I got on the Internet and looked it up. Soulmate – One of two persons compatible with each other in disposition, point of view or sensitivity and a person who is perfectly suited to another in temperament, a person who resembles another in attitudes and beliefs.

A few days went by and I pondered was the voice saying soulmate referring to Tristan. It had to be referring to Tristan because my boyfriend definitely did not have a temperament similar to mine or a similar point of view. One morning, I clocked into work at 8:00 a.m. I was filing books away in the department that had been left by patrons from the night before. Lea, the receptionist for the archaeological area, said the word, "Soulmate." Now I had not said anything to anyone about the word "Soulmate" so how did she know to say that word. All I do know is that she reads her Bible daily, speaks in tongues, goes to church and serves the Lord. When I heard her say "Soulmate", I walked to where she was sitting. Lea said, "Sometimes, your soulmate can be in a relationship when you meet them." She also said that when you meet them your whole countenance would change, and that they would love your child just as much as they love you." I said, "I think I might know who it is. The next time Tristan saw me he said, "Nice to see you again." I was sitting at my desk where I had told him through a letter that I would be shining bright as the sun on the inside as he walked by.

Around 12:05, I went to lunch. I entered the café and what do you know. There he was and he said, "Go ahead, I'm waiting for the grill. I shyly grabbed a plate, and got three vegetables. The cook handed him his order and he walked on in front of me to the cashier. It was almost as if he forgot I was standing a little way off, but somewhat behind. He turned around and looked at me as if he said, "Gosh, she's kinda cute. She is interested in me, huh? She told me I was a real man, and that she had never met a real man before." I was looking at the ceiling as someone was pointing out something. When I looked over in his direction, our eyes met from a ways across the room. I had already told him I did not want anyone to think there might be something going on between the two of us.

I wrote in my diary later that evening. . . . I walked into the café, and there he is. He says, "Go on, I'm waiting for the grill." I gingerly grab a plate and proceed to get corn, peas and broccoli. He stands to the side of the others and gives one a shoulder massage. He knows I'm looking, and I thought he was just showing me that he always does that sort of thing and nothing is meant by it, particularly the time when he put his arm around my shoulder when we seemed to feel the same about the cafeteria food. But as if he forgot I was looking, he shyly looked back at me, while the cashier was giving him his change. He looked like he said to himself, "Huh, she is my Secret Admirer. I'm a real man, (She told me so in a letter through the mail, even though she may or may not see me again. I only see her once every two weeks. I feel like I have been here for everybody else, but no one has been here for me.)

Chapter 4

Alpha male

I woke up one morning and lie there quiet for a bit thinking of Tristan and getting ready to rise to tackle my day. The Holy Spirit said, "Alpha male." I said out loud, "Alpha male? What is that? I came to the conclusion that I would look this word up too so maybe this would lead me to find out who the soulmate was. I eagerly and with some expectation got up out of bed, went in the living room and turned on the computer. I brought up the Internet and put in the word "alpha male." It gave a definition of someone who fit the traits of Tristan, and the criteria surely did not fit anyone else. It said alpha males have personality, they are confident, driven, and often times successful. In other words, "The big man on campus." It also said that they may come across as kind of feminine but I knew from his smile that he wasn't.

The next time I went to work, Tristan was definitely avoiding me. I heard his voice, but I did not see him. It seemed he avoided me the whole day. I never saw his face. I phoned his department, but he had already left for the day. I had never experienced liking someone this much in the past. In fact, I had a fiancé while in college in Virginia, but

I still had managed to maintain an "A" average. Maybe this experience was different because I am a woman now, and not a girl. I am a woman in years, wisdom and survival. Maybe it was because Tristan was a real man. I wondered whether he could come shoot some hoops, some Make 'Em, Take 'Em or maybe we could meet me at the zoo. Even meet me at the Annual Corporate Spelling Bee which was April 20th. The next time my weekend to work arrived, I only had a few carts of books to shelve. I still felt Tristan was avoiding me but I was not sure. I just could not resist at least calling to say, "Hi" on that weekend. Things did seem kind of slow that day and awfully quiet as the elevator seemed louder. It was spring break for the City Schools. When I called, the person who answered the phone asked, "May I ask who is calling?" The person beckoned Tristan to the phone and he answered oddly. He seemed agitated, as if to say, "What are you calling me for?" I tried to ignore it, even though it caught me off guard. I asked, "What are you doing?" He said," Working hard as usual." His tone seemed rough. I thought maybe he was tired and he did seem to be avoiding me. I truly want to get to know him, everything about him. You know the old 100 questions, but because I am driving while talking on the cell phone for the first time, I got a little tongue-tied. Tristan, tired of the silence, asks abruptly, "CAN I HELP YOU WITH SOMETHING?" This really caught me off guard, so I timidly, quietly said, "No. I'm sorry to have bothered you." Tristan strongly said, "You have a nice day." I wanted to call and banter back, but I decided against it. Maybe I was wrong about this man. I came to the conclusion that either he did not like me the least bit, or that I had struck some cord in him, and he was putting up his defenses. I had never been on the receiving end of such behavior, but I accepted it. Sometimes you have to realize a man can love his children and want for his children more than to be with the most intriguing woman he's ever seen in his life who is interested in him. Not outstanding of what kind of person he really is, but just that can sometimes make the attraction stronger. I went about my evening at my new place. Later that night, I found that sleep eluded me. I kept thinking about him. Evidently, there must be somebody else when he said he could speak to me while we were at the facility and I had called him to ask did he have an email address or phone number I could call to chat with him. I wonder if he is sleeping well. I surmised that he probably is after working all weekend. I asked God to help me stop thinking about him, and I said a prayer for Tristan hoping that someone would come and fill a position alongside him so he wouldn't have to work so hard. Looking at the type of man he is, I had come up with the answer to why my Aunt Ruby cried at her husband, George's funeral. I had wondered about it 10 years, and now know the answer. It was because he must have been really good to her. The answer was so simple now, but it could not have been arrived upon earlier after seeing my father not comfort my mother, Evelina when the matriarch, Beulah, had passed away when I was in the second or third grade.

On Sunday morning, I woke up and felt miserable about what had transpired the night before on the phone with Tristan. I had noticed three calls from a particular number and I felt it might be him calling. Because of his avoiding me, I started to hate everything about myself. Everything. The way I caught footballs with my brother and his friends. I regretted my personality, the way I looked, who my old boyfriends were, some guys I never gave the chance, those who wanted me to leave my Mom before I was ready. It is evident that I did not make a good choice when I have to talk to Bellows Creek as if he is 2-years old, his not believing in himself, lazy, selfish. A man will die for his wife and child. As I sat I remembered the day when I thought about what M-A-N in his right mind would keep someone from teaching their child how to operate in the world. Emphasis on the word M-A-N and emphasis on In His Right Mind.

I know Tristan should be off limits because he already has someone even though he did not directly say it. I had already done that one time before, dating a man that already had a girlfriend in his home state, and the relationship was not good. Furthermore, it seems everyone has kids they are not ready for and is dealing with a partner who is ill-equipped and just boring, but just to even think of Tristan gives me a buoyant feeling. I am wondering if he feels something too -- the reason why he is avoiding me. I, myself, would not go out of my way to keep someone that had a crush on me from seeing me. Surely he isn't that juvenile. Maybe he does feel something. Perhaps he is trying to stay away and is snappy because he knows he could be with me if his situation was different. This weekend I am really going to have to grit my teeth and resist calling him, but with the way I feel it is going to be hard.

As I write I remember the Pastor said that God wants us to worship him in Spirit and in Truth. I believed that the Spirit was not referring to any actress or celebrity, and it turned out I was correct. Coretta Scott King passed away and I knew then she was the significant one the Holy Spirit was referring to who was going to pass away after Christmas. She passed on January 30, 2006. With my Mom's death, death of Rosa Parks, the mother of Civil Rights Movement and the drum majorette's passing, I had wrote in my journal that I felt like a motherless child.

It is evident that Eros (God of Love) has delivered a pleasantly lethal bite. I have never met anyone like him. At times I can't even sleep. This not being able to sleep business should have happened when I was much younger, first dating. It leads me to believe maybe it is love, but how can it be, when it is definitely unrequited. I decided I had to use the light that he provided as a catalyst to keep me glowing. I had not been this joyful, or optimistic in years. Because he was still on my mind, I decided I wouldn't send my story, Thanksgivens, but would send the story My Monster (written as if my kitten, Simba i.e. Nurse doodles, Semeenemee) was doing the writing. I feel that I really care for Tristan. I mean really care, and just my luck I can't have him. It feels like a nightmare. I've got to be dreaming but it's my life, and it's true. It's just as profound as waking up and finding there are zombies except there are no monsters, just an emptiness that I've felt twice when trying to let him go, but a feeling I never want to experience again. It actually feels like a part of me has died twice, and I do not want to get so wrapped in my feelings for him again that I have those feelings of condemnation in the pit of my stomach after lying prostrate and asking God for His forgiveness. I kept thinking about what I did to deserve someone that would treat me the way my beau had. He was despicable towards me. I just don't know how I mustered the strength not to fight back in the same way, but the Bible says, "Vengeance is mine. I will repay (not in that order). Every time school would start in the Fall it would pretty much seal my fate in staying, keeping the family together, trying to make it work, thinking that he will change. I kept forgiving over and over.

The treatment got worse and worse, until there was despair and giving up on God. A year after my mother died, I wouldn't even go out in the sun, not even on the front porch. I just stayed inside lying in bed with the light on all night, not falling asleep until the 5:00 a.m. prayer on the radio was complete. I feel that maybe if my father would have started his day by praying, and believing that prayer and accepting, he could have had a better relationship with my mother.

I went for a ride after stopping at the Chinese restaurant for a soda. I couldn't help but grin, smile and laugh about that song, "Ain't No Other Man" by Christina Aguilera. The lyrics of that song was picturesque in Tristan's case. I was so impressed with Tristan that I decided to start writing a story. I remember I had wagered to tell only one coworker that I was writing a story, and he said to write the story clean because it is a testimony. But I do not want the testimony, I want Tristan. I put my head on the back of my seat and started to cry, but I told myself to stop because it was going to impact the way I look, putting bags under my eyes, tears coming from my heart and soul. I wish now I was emotionless. I asked myself, "Why didn't Ma make me go back to church when I got upset when the pastor chided me." Maybe she did not make me go back to church because she met my father while she was in church, and he turned into a Hound of Hell. I rehearsed in my mind again about what had gone wrong. I thought about asking him out. I was a little nervous and scared that he would turn me down. Even though he is a man, why wasn't he mature enough to say what he really felt? Why couldn't he say he was committed early on? Could it be that I may be a good catch? My first boyfriend used to call me gorgeous when I would get angry, but I never paid any attention to that. My coworkers used to call me Grandma when I used to work periodically at the Smith and Welton warehouse while attending college, getting those Easter dresses tagged and loaded on delivery trucks. In my mid 20's Brian used to call me fly girl, but I was real, nothing fake about me. I never believed anything anyone told me about my looks. I had strived to control everything in my life, and to live for 42 years and run into my twin, a male, my twin flame, is overwhelming. We are about the same skin tone, but he is about 8 inches taller. We both have broad shoulders, mine femininely so. We both have long legs. My inseam on me is just as tall as his is on him. Incidentally we both drive the same color vehicle, and both wear black eyeglasses. Gosh, really, is he a soul mate or is he a twin flame that did notice me? I need to forgive myself for what I did but if I had not, I wouldn't have been given these flowers, this bouquet. A bouquet of energy, third eye opening, hearing better, understanding Jesus and his sacrifice—how he gave up his heavenly/earthly body so that I could be saved, and not separated from my Heavenly Father, and how God loves us so much as his children that even as we stumble, fall and bruise our knees, he picks us up, dusts us off, kisses the bruise and says lovingly over and over, "Go try again and keep trying until you get it right." The only thing is I know I've got it now but it's really lonely not having anyone to share that I've got it with. It's hard when you've been walking around alone in a relationship and felt that if another man hits me, I do not know what I may do.

Again, my thoughts travel to my mother and how she may have thought, "God, why have thy forsaken me?" I felt that maybe my mother told Aunt Susie or even Ms. Nellie how her husband, my father, was treating her. Later on that evening after baking cookies for the ballet class I was teaching at the community center I pondered about how I felt about myself and what I have gone through. I was being abused, but yet my daughter was Valedictorian of the middle school. I am either weak in my strength or strong in my weakness. Are they the same or are they different? I did not have the sticker for the correct year on my car displaying that it had been inspected. MPD caught me going down the street to pick up Esprit from school. It was a female cop. I told her what had been going on, what I had endured and she let me go without giving me a ticket. Anyway, I know deep down its TIME. I am going to make sure my dancers dance at church, start mailing my things home, get Esprit's school records and get ready to ride the bus back to Norfolk. I have not really met anyone else besides Marvin, but while Marvin is sweet, kind of reserved, I kind of feel he is not the right guy for me. I need a "man's man" because I am a woman's woman. Marvin seemed nice, would give Laura a hug at work, but seemed to hug her just to appease her. I would always move out of their way and give them space. Remember, I had already experienced a bad relationship when dating someone who had a special person in another state.

On Monday after taking Esprit to school, I stopped in at the store and bought yogurt, apples and bananas. I sat in the car and reasoned about why I am giving up on my beau. I asked, "Am I supposed to keep carrying him especially with him hitting on me? He poked me in my surgery site just like they showed on Passion of the Christ when the soldier pierces Jesus' side with that spear-like object. Every time my beau hit me it was like a blow to my spirit. It took a long time for me to realize it was really over…. it seems before it started. The reasons why I stayed were varied. First it was that I cared for him so I tried again -- mistakenly never minding self-preservation. Then it was the baby crying, "I want my Daddy" and caring about the child's

mental stability. Then it was "I want my Momma." Then, as you know, summers were good, but once school let back in in the Fall, I stayed until school ended. I kept trying and trying. I guess my daughter thinks, "How can she still laugh? How can she dance? It is God and his power that is holding me. I have never done anything to hurt anyone intentionally but it just seems I've been railroaded. Sometimes I feel I could just lie down and die. But I'm ready now. Ready to go back home.

Esprit thinks her father was in the Coast Guard. This so called man did not do what he was supposed to do. He wouldn't get a job painting when he had the chance. He wouldn't ride with the guy next door on the truck to do construction work, the guy offered him a ride in his truck. He also refused to go into the Coast Guard saying, "I'm not going in the Coast Guard for you or anybody else" when I literally begged and groveled that he go into the Coast Guard to help me with the bills. He would not sell cars, go paint (the guy said he could ride with him in the morning) nothing. My father said, "What kind of Man is going to let the woman take care of him. The man is supposed to take care of the woman, lead and take care of his family. Later on that day after picking up Esprit at school, I needed something from the store. I looked into oncoming traffic and it was Tristan, going in the opposite direction. I was exasperated. I asked myself, "Why do I keep seeing him, does it mean something? But life is not fair, and will I find someone who I'd rather be with other than Tristan? I reasoned to myself once again, if he is not married, he is fair game. I wondered if I should write him a note that would say….It is evident that there must be a lot going on in your life right now the way I unintentionally, but unmistakably upset you the other day when I called. I was driving while talking on the cellphone (first time, last time). I will accept a date with you the week of my birthday as an apology. Remember I said I would like some interesting conversation and two lemonades, 2 coffees, 2 hot chocolates, whatever your fancy. Hold Up. Stop It! I reasoned that if he was interested, he would not be hiding from me, and he certainly would not have acted that way on the phone. It sure is funny how some people's lives are full of epiphanies; revelations and others' lives are just ….

But I still feel that he might be my soul mate, and just because he is in a relationship it does not mean she is the right woman for him. That is what has happened. We were so busy being "grown" …. later finding that the father/mother is not the best equipped to be a suitable meet. Yes, meet, not mate. (Maybe the word should be soul meet.) I wonder if he is really happy. I know I am not!

A few days later, I was driving through the neighborhood, and the Laotian girls hollered and waved as I drove by, but something told me to go back. I went back to see what was up, and they told me about a little girl who lived at the Brook Apartments who needed to be picked up from daycare or her mother would be assessed late charges. I said, "Come on, Let's go." They got into my car and we drove across the interstate to the day care center. When they got inside the daycare center, they walked with one of the lead teachers. A little girl was going out the door and as is customary with me, I would always tell children to tie their shoes or it would launch them forward like a missile and they would fall hard. I have had to do this countless times as if the children's mothers do not care about what happens to them and not tell them to keep their shoes tied. Also I witness the kids standing in the grocery carts, and one tumble out of the basket could render a major head injury or death. In fact, I already have imagined the sound of the head hitting the store floor. Anyhow, I told the little girl whose shoe I was tying that one of my classmates had taught me how to tie my shoe. When I went outside to find the Laotian girls, I asked where was the child I was supposed to be taking home and it turns out it was the same little girl whose shoe I had tied. The little girl's cousin was there to ride her across the interstate on the middle bar of the bike and I said, "No, no!" I opened the back door of the car, buckled the little girl in and rode back across the Interstate.

I felt good to have done that, but then at night I feel kind of inadequate because I am not with Tristan,

I began writing my story after finding out the Queen of Sheba's name was Makeda and she is the woman talked about in the Bible in the chapter Song of Songs. I wrote my story with some of Song of Songs in it comparing it to my looking for Tristan at the basketball court?" In my mind I answered my own question, "Because I saw his soul through his eyes." I thought I would ask him if his wife had ever seen his soul. I quickly felt let down again and asked myself, "What difference does it make? We still cannot be together."

I woke up at 6:15 a.m. I do not need an alarm clock. Jesus wakes me up on time. It seems I wake up every morning when it is time for Tristan to go to work or on the weekends when he is just about to walk in the door of the facility. After I dropped off Esprit for school, I went to the store for fruit to continue on my diet. When I pulled into the parking space, I laid my head back on the headrest and wondered if my daughter would really be alright when I am gone. I thought about my mother and how, almost at the end of her struggle she was more than furious with my father. I said to myself, You….." I sometimes think about how Esprit will do when I am gone? I feel that I have made a mistake with dating this man. I felt that surely someone close to me in age would have the same drive, motivation and spirit but I found that he did not. This man is a user, a life-taker, a spirit breaker. He does just enough, and that is it. Well, just enough isn't going to get it, and does not get it--not "Coming from where I'm from" Anthony Hamilton. I remember all of the orders for donuts I had trying to go on a trip to Six Flags over Georgia while attending Vocational Technical school. I sold 110 boxes of donuts. In fact I had to get the money for them first. I hand-delivered each box all by myself. My teacher, Ms. Batten, loaded her car and took me home after classes ended at VoTech that day. Nevertheless the trip was never realized.

The trip was canceled because only a small number of people had sold enough to go on the trip but it was not enough. I was disappointed that we did not get to go to Six Flags over Georgia. Also I was the captain of the majorette squad in junior high and high school. I was responsible for the choreography, the pompoms, the boots, and the corsages for homecoming and with my mother's help, I did just that. I surmised that this man may have kids as I have a daughter, and how there is no way that I am going to get him away from them because he loves them so much, but still I think about him on awakening, during the day and sometimes halting my sleep. I even think that sometimes I cannot sleep because he is not asleep yet, and that I am awake when he is awake. I took French in junior high school but let it go because I lost my basics. However, with the influx of Latinos in the Mid-South, I fittingly learned what sounds like "hola" (meaning "hello") and an endearing phrase of Spanish to whisper in Tristan's ear if I could ever get close to him.

Later that evening, I found I was so wired up from the world and my thoughts that I could not sleep and thought of Tristan and I as King and Queen, relaxing shoulder to shoulder.

At 9:30 a.m. Monday morning, I went to my computer to set up for the day with the Services company. As the tech ran down a list of things to check off, I realized I was saying, "check" as if we were going through the checklist to take off in a ship. I told him I never watched Star Wars nor Star Trek. I would always watch the horror movie where there was a monster and there would be a team of annihilators. These shows showed cooperation between the Captain and his shipmates. Breathing and the rhythm of the words (mine and the tech's cooperating through communication) reminded me how I felt what I saw of Tristan on that commercial about the facility. He seemed to do his work effortlessly and with such care and patience as if he were saying, "I'm here. I will do my best to take good care of you." His personality showed through saying everything is right with the world. As I think about him, I come to the conclusion that he is not fake. I feel it in my heart that the way he acts is not fake, and that this is how he feels. This is how he really feels. He has to feel this way to do well on his job. The work day can be kind of enjoyable if you do your best and let spirit be your wings for the day -- spirit in your walk, spirit in your talk, spirit in the way you drive, spirit in the way you move that says, "Have feet, Will travel!

After coming home from school Esprit asked me for a hug. Esprit and I were standing in the kitchen, and Esprit decided she wanted to see how tall she was compared to me, barefoot. I measured Esprit against my forehead, and was a little concerned, teasingly so though, that my daughter was taller than me. It looked kind of close. I told Esprit to take off her tennis shoes. It really was close. Esprit said, "Dang! Tsk! Almost there." I told Esprit that her diet has a lot to do with how she grows and that may be she should drink more milk. Esprit fixed herself some stuffing and fried chicken. As she tried to run to my room, I told Esprit to fix me a plate also. After a tiring day, I started thinking about Tristan again. There's a thin line between love and hate. I hated the relationship my father and mother had but was excited about what could be with Tristan. Tristan probably hates what he sees in me because a female, his mother, is what secured his journey to Earth, but also loves what he sees in me – my fortitude, energy, perseverance and faith. So today was the day I finally got a handle on my feelings for Tristan even though he provided "the light" to make me realize who I am, what I am…a strong black woman. I had taunted with having him, not having him, wanting him to be responsible, wanting him to be carefree. The Internet says men thrive on financial status, adventure and freedom. I have been looking for someone like Tristan all my life. The reason I had not found him was because neither of us were really ready, and because we had not met yet. On Monday when I finally returned home from my errands, I looked at the answering machine and still no one had called.

On Friday, someone called at 6:32 p.m., did not say anything and just listened. Even though Easter Sunday is this Sunday and Roots is coming on, I am still going to send Tristan the packet. I wonder if I missed him again. It seems like it is so hard to get to him. As I look out of Esprit's window, the sun was shining, but tears fell from my eyes because it seems Tristan and I will never be together. I look at the end of the building where my King could come walking knowing full well Tristan will never come around that corner. Later on after getting mad with Esprit for not wanting to go into the kitchen to check to see if the trash had been taken out, I ended up walking around that edge of the apartment building myself. As I walk, my head is held too high. I am not friendly and looking at everyone. I am walking like I wish someone would get in my way. This is not like me. I was always a little tomboyish but now I am walking with bravado. I know for a fact Tristan has changed because of what has happened. I really did not come down to the Mid-South to start any trouble. I met someone who I really liked and really care for. I think his significant other will not even let him have the vehicle now. Maybe I will let him know everything that happened, but then he will make up his mind again that he would rather be with his significant other. Even though I found him, and I feel he deserves to be with me, I still feel he might not be the right one. Just think of it …If you meet someone who caused you to know what the word "swoon" means, put a pep in your step, showed heart, strength, personality, seemingly interesting to talk to, and got it going on, could you really let them go? Just not even try to make him yours? Plus an added plus is that you really feel they are your soulmate? Anyway, in the course of it all, we let go of one another so we may be with each other again in this life or the next whether it is a father, mother, dear brother or sister, baby's daddy, baby's mama and even friends and significant others. Unfortunately, but fortunately every morning we are completing what our parents have started for us and for those of us who have children we are finishing what we have started for them, all the while cursing and sometimes loving the choices we have made along the way.

I am so enamored with Tristan that I assume he rides the bus and I stopped at the main bus terminal on American Way and sat there in the car a while to see if he was going to get off the bus to transfer or something. I even paid attention to the bus stops that I thought he may take to get to work so I could give him a ride.

I do not know why I think of it at this time but it is true what Jackson said in the 1980s, when the Norfolk Public Schools' students went to see him in an assembly. "That anything you believe, you can achieve", and that we are "Somebody" and lastly that it's all about your choices. I knew that I controlled my life today in that I only had one child, Esprit, and that I needed Tristan's light, fight and God's grace to push me on even if I ended up back home in Virginia. I knew the next six months were very crucial that would end in October, and to be strong as best I could. I still sometimes get the feeling Tristan has no interest in me and every time night falls I may not see or talk with him again even though that just might be the right thing, but friends tell me to think positive. I thought about the home he shares with his significant other. My home surely was not with all the manipulating, hitting, etc. With this realization, I knew I was correct in getting out of this relationship. When thinking back in time a little, I felt like calling my childhood friend.

The next day I woke up at 5:30 a.m. and Eros visited again. This time it was in my heart. I went to work to eat lunch that day. One of my coworkers said there were many places to eat here in the Mid-South and why did I have to pick there to eat and on a Saturday too.

It's now 12:10. The lunchroom closes at 1:00. I am wondering if he's coming to the cafeteria to eat today. I'm waiting to give him my story, but he did not come near the café that day and I hear Renia talking loudly to a male coworker and he said something like… He is where he wants to be and because the young lady did not holler back, he's gone. I said to myself Well, I'm hollering, waiting, writing letters, sending cards and still no results. I think I have my answer. He won't even talk to me.

On Sunday I did not see him. He did not call me and I did not call him. He will not talk to me. I can't do this anymore, I can't. There must be someone else out there for me because it's definitely not him. I'm still driving down to the Mount Olive basketball courts looking for Tristan, but he's never there. He is more mature than these guys, maybe even older, and he's definitely not looking for me." I sent a card for Easter, and a small note apologizing for my actions. I can't help but wonder does he like this – all the notes and cards? After I give him my story, I can't, won't say anything else. He has to come to me, call me while I am here or write me. What is the use of giving him my cellphone number when he won't even talk to me? I just would like to know why he said he would chat with me while he was here. Sometimes the quietest guys can be the biggest players, and he won't talk to me, but he is not a player. I really do wonder why he never confirmed my assumption that there was a significant other or is it that he really is interested in me, I did start writing him in October and I care for him. I am inside of what love is with him. I do not know what to think and I have been interviewing male colleagues. It seems that whether they have a girlfriend or wife is not anyone's business and they would never divulge such. Ah ha! So that is how it is.

The next day, I went to work. I knew he was there because they called his name over the intercom. However, it was just like I thought; he was either avoiding me or just did not give a darn. I got the story together as best I could. I wanted the pages that were not as grammatically correct clear, at least, neat, so I typed those. When I got courageously mad, I put the story in an envelope, and went to his office to give it to him. Uh Oh! There was a woman in the office I had never seen before. Could this be the significant other? I did not leave the story.

I went home and was kind of disappointed that I could not give him the story today. However, I said to myself I cannot go another week or two weeks like this. "This brother is going to tell me something straight." He is going to either tell me to leave him alone, he is not interested or let me know that he has someone else. I kind of suspected she may be kinda special because I could not call him or email him at home, but his charm, personality, nobleness, strength and manliness held me. I finally got the nerve to call, and he said, "Hi, Athena." I said, "I finished my story, the story about us that I mentioned to you that I wrote through my letters to you. Would you like to read it so you can give me some feedback on it?" He said he was very flattered, but that he was in a committed relationship. I said, "When were you going to tell me? I said, "I guess I'll see you around then. He apologized for sounding abrupt on the phone that day when he said, "MAY I HELP YOU WITH SOMETHING? He said it was the dynamics of the job and that he was not trying to be rude that day on the phone. I had written that I cared for him. He inspired me to be a "Natural Woman" again...... strong, confident, phenomenal, a woman that I always was but my boyfriend had dimmed that light for so many years that only the memory of my mother, the life of my daughter kept me going until I saw this fine young man doing his job, being respectful, cheerful, strong, everything positive, and it in turn brought out the best in me. He said, "You have a nice holiday." I said, "You, too." I was happy that we had this understanding, and that he is just what I thought – very kind and sweet. I said out loud with no one else in the room, "Darn. Uh, uh, uh." Again, I say to myself, I don't know who she is, but she is a lucky girl. Exasperatingly, I asked God where is and who is my . . .

I wrote Tristan another letter.

> *"Hey,*
>
> *I know you told me you are in a committed relationship, and that you were flattered. I wanted to let you know that I was going to ask you to be on my team for the Corporate Spelling Bee which is next week; however, I never got around to asking you. What kind of books do you read? What is your mother's name? How many sisters and brothers do you have? What is your father's name? Do you know how or why you were named Tristan? Did you play ball in school? What year did you graduate? What college did you go to? Were you born in Tennessee? How many kids do you have? Are your parents still living? Are you an only child? Middle child like*

me? But I never got the chance to ask you. This to me is getting to know you longitudinally and latitude, may be one day I will. This little escapade we had made me very happy. I believe you were too. I felt at peace for the first time in a very long time. I want you to know I'm not a loose woman. I've been with one guy for 18 years, but that relationship is history. They say knight in shining armor; I say "light" in shining armor.

Athena

Later on that week, I was still thinking about him. I could not sleep. He sure has got to be in love with this girl to push away someone like me, but I care about him. What do I do? Keep my distance; try to learn more about him when I go to work every two weeks when he is there? I've got to stay here so I can keep an eye out on him. I received a call from my supervisor asking me to come in the next day to discuss some things. I had just had my evaluation so I kind of wondered could it have been something about Tristan. I went to the store to pick up a few things and while walking in the parking lot I felt a little odd. Something was not right, but I did not know exactly what it was at the time. The day I went to the facility, my supervisor called me to the office and then we walked over to Human Resources. She asked me what was going on. She said Tristan was taken aback. I was slightly embarrassed but I owned up to everything. I said I had been sending letters and cards to Tristan since October but we had never touched. The last letter was sent in April. The letter said,

"Tristan,

I don't know where you are right now (it seems like you are always at work). I have been looking for you all week at the basketball

court on Mt. Olive. I am your soul mate. I am everything you ever wanted and needed. The Holy Spirit uttered the word "Soulmate" one night when I was thinking about you. In October last year when I started feeling you, you were a light to me. I started exercising, my skin got softer, and I felt joy. You gave me strength in your strength, my lips got pinker. I've written a story called A and T. I started it in late March. It is not made up, you'll see. We (you and I) have lived it. I have been your friend since October; you have been my life, my milk and honey and my light. She said my soul mate would love my child as if it were his own. I wonder how many children WE have. My daughter is going to high school in the fall. I never got a chance to ask you how many kids do you have Tristan? I care for you. I've been looking for you all my life and on Christmas, I know I Touched A Dream (The Dells 1971) because you were my light. You're my soul mate.

Athena

The big boss went on to say she did not understand; Tristan is married! I said he did not tell me. The big boss said he did not have to tell. I thought to myself that if someone said that they admire you, and said that they were shining bright as the sun on the inside as you walked by that you had no idea that the person was developing feelings for you and you would not tell the person you had a significant other. I told her that I do not have any friends or family here as I am from Virginia. I did not tell them how Tristan made me feel – how he was more man than I had ever seen. How I felt joyful, happy, just felt great and that everything was right with the world even though we were not together. After being suspended from where my "light" worked, I was very upset. I could not understand that instead of coming to me, he went and told the boss. Doesn't he know that I am really his soul sister, and that he should have come to me? He didn't bother to look at the dates of the letters.

They were delivered before our conversation on the phone where he seemed like he was sorry; Well, he apologized. I felt that we had an understanding, and in the end I felt that he was very sweet. I felt betrayed by the world and knew this was the end of the relationship; I cried. I just could not believe that he would go to these lengths to get me suspended, but I guess a man has got to do what a man has got to do, but is he really a man when he needs a woman to do his battling for him? When he talked to me on the phone Easter Sunday, he still seemed like he needed to search for the word he was trying to say. Why couldn't he just say, "I'm married." Instead he said, "I'm in a committed relationship." Committed relationship means to be in a relationship because of morals. It does not mean you took a vow. I was in a committed relationship wherein the guy gave me a promise ring. I surmise that now since I am older it was a promise to get engaged, not a promise for marriage, but he broke that promise over 18 years ago. I feel that if a person is married "Darn it, just say it, and be proud of it. If you have eight kids at home "Darn it, say it, and be proud of it. Why be ashamed? I chalked all of this up to a learning experience; that I am aggressive and a go-getter. Evidently for Tristan to cause so much hurt to me and my daughter, he must have gotten fed up with the whole thing. Maybe now he will wear his wedding ring; and may be next time it seems like someone is trying to get close to him, he needs to speak up and say that he is married or…. maybe he just did not want to hurt my feelings so he just did not say anything. I thought so much about the whole calamity that I could not get good concentration on my work and developed a headache. Did he think I was going to hurt him? No, no, I would not hurt a fly. Just last summer I scooped up a little kitten that was suffering in the hot sun behind the back left wheel of a car, and drove even almost to the point of running out of gas to secure a place for the kitten, which I named Heaven, to receive help. Espin named him Miracle. We finally got the black and white kitten to an animal hospital that would accept him, and they told us after they checked him out that he would have to be euthanized; he was too far gone.

I thought about Tristan hoping he wouldn't do anything to hurt himself because he got me into trouble, prayed to God that he wouldn't try to hurt himself and that he remember the words in my letter that he has mettle. It's hard caring for a man you can't be around and can't see anymore. God? Why do I have to go through this? I am really hurt. I whimper-cried quietly in the bathroom because I knew I would never see him again. I wished I had never met him and I came to the conclusion that he probably wished that too. I thought to myself, "God, why was Tristan born?" and I deemed that he probably was thinking the same thing about me, God, was she born to test me? On Monday, I was still reeling from the situation that Tristan got me suspended and could not even dance or exercise. Was he jealous of all the things that I had done – being a majorette co-captain at the high school while in junior high, a ballet dancer as an adult, competed in college dance girl tryouts, and a camouflage belt in Tae Kwon Do? Was he jealous of me because it seemed that I had a good upbringing; maybe he is a foster child?

The next day, I was sitting at my computer and the first ladybug of the season flew in. I remembered that my mother had shown me and my sister when we were ages 3 and 5 years old, a ladybug. It was in Southampton County, Virginia. I even remember the ladybug was on a light green leaf. A second time during the day while sitting in my work chair at my computer, a ladybug visited and again about 7 p.m. a ladybug visited for the last time that day. I thought odd that the ladybug visited three times and I said to myself, I must be getting close to my answer as that was a Trinity. The day before when I was out at the elementary school parking lot dancing, I met Tina Athena and daughter's name is Esprit Athena. Three Athenas together. I ascertained that I must be getting close to this whole situation resolving—that this Trinity was some kind of sign.

Later on that night I packed my things to go to give the CD to Tristan, and on the way, even getting gas I felt like I was not supposed to be out there, and I did not feel safe living on my own, but I had to maintain a positive attitude, a strong attitude. On Sunday, I got up and went to church. As I entered the sanctuary, I felt ashamed at what I had done. Through the Word of God on that day, I realized God still loved me and that some kind of way whether love for his family, himself or for God, this time Tristan (Adam) prevailed. I still felt that Tristan could have let me know he was spoken for, but he didn't. He must have been trying to keep harmony in the workplace but evidently he could not take it anymore and had to do what he needed to do for his own sanity. I realized that his spouse and children may well be in this church, and that I would never want him to leave his wife because she "put on a few pounds" or whatever, but only leave if they cannot get along anymore and that favorably and amicably they could part. I had developed an emotional connection to him because he was confident, and because of his essence (spirit) I internalized the song, *"This Is For The Very Best in You"* – *Change.*

On Saturday night after work, I decided to go out to the club. Once I pulled into the parking lot, I almost cried. I have to be out in this type of crowd again. I decided that I did not want to do this, and went home. Later on that night, I was still thinking about the situation and pondered to myself that Tristan was trying to act honest and everything like he had not done anything. But, then again… it's all my fault. Well, the first thing is I should not have ever called him. The second thing is when I called to ask could I chat with him, he should have said then that he was married even though my relationship was definitely over in the physical sense since 1998, but I had tried to make it work to no avail. As it stands the relationship is over.

I had endured so much in this relationship. He said that he was going to push me out of the house, naked; he told me he was going to "mess me up" if anything happened to his daughter. He had even told me one day I looked like I had on a casket dress because I had put on a few pounds. In all he probably deserved …. but somehow I had maintained not to do anything to get him back. I prayed the Serenity Prayer and asked God to help me accept that I cannot have Tristan. He is married and let no man/woman put asunder.

On Monday, I was happy, but I felt an emptiness. I realized that in the course of time that what happened to me could happen again but maybe only twice in the facility's lifetime. I realized and deduced that another female, a student at the university, and working at the Naval Base Pier restaurant in VA would meet someone off of a ship, have a child, go through Hell and be blessed to meet someone like Tristan. I asked God why this had to happen to me. The object was to get to know Tristan better, not begin to deeply care for him. As I sit at my desk typing, the sun is shining directly on me from the window. I remember that in 1999 that I wouldn't/couldn't go outside because of my mother's death and I not wanting the sun shine on me because I was so depressed. I would lie in bed all night and could not sleep until the 5:00 a.m. morning prayer was complete. I remember I had told Tristan I would be shining bright as the sun on the inside when he walked by my workspace and not to feel upset if I did not acknowledge his presence overtly to make sure no one thought that something was going on. I said to myself, "I'm wondering if this is the reason why he never told me he was married. Darn, so in a way this is my fault." Still this does not make me not miss him, and long for him any less.

Later on that evening, I looked in the bathroom mirror as if I was looking at Tristan for some understanding. I almost feel that when he looks in the mirror at himself, he sees me too, and interjects that he was sorry, but "take no prisoners." The next day I gathered my references and emailed them to Nancie at the Physical Therapy Center. I wrote this letter:

Tristan,

I'm not going to let you and Sharon take something beautiful and turn it into something ugly. Just you at your best, doing your job, acting respectful, seemingly cheerful, and having good character made me internalize the song, "This Is For the Very Best In You" – Change, and from how I felt about myself (joyful, happy, having more faith, strength), it gave me the courage and faith to get out of a tumultuous relationship. That is how I began to care for you.

All is forgiven.

Athena

On Friday, I took Esprit to school, went and shot some hoops, danced and then went to get my eyelashes and eyebrows done. At the beauty salon, the cosmetology student asked my name and I said, "Athena" and the she said, "Ooooh, I like that." She went on to talk about her boyfriend. She said she met him when he didn't know anyone here, did not know his way around – just to work and home and that he has a kid, she has a kid, and that they want one together. I said in a joking manner, "Don't have anymore." We both laughed.

Thinking about that day again in the café, I feel I saw his soul on that day, and he saw mine. Through our eyes, our souls were communicating, I thought about how I "chased" him, not by foot, but by phone. He had been hiding from me since the week after Valentine's Day, and I wouldn't leave him alone just like those women chasing Benny Hill on late night TV. I realize that right now he may be still at work and would not find that funny at all.

However, if the Change CD comes in the mail, I'll make sure that he gets it, and maybe for my birthday I'll send him two stories. I am beginning to accept that it is finished. I was a little disappointed that it looked as though I may have to go see the Boogie Body Band alone as I had already asked my coworkers if we could get together to go see the Boogie Body Band. We used to listen to the Boogie Body Band on the radio when we were young. On Monday morning when I picked up my daughter, an ambulance rode by with its sirens wailing, and I thought about Tristan. I had to believe Tristan was okay. I care for him. Later on that morning, I watched Divorce Court starring the Judge . I had not watched in over a month. Just so happens that day's court case was about a domineering husband. The Judge told the husband that his wife could be covered from head to toe and a man can find her desirable because it comes from the heart. Everyone clapped and when the case ended, the Judge stood up and while in her chambers gave kudos to herself that she looked good also. I had to laugh but I did pay attention to what she said. The weekend arrived.

I woke, took a shower and dressed in a pair of flared jeans, a beige off the shoulder sparkling corset top and a cropped jean jacket. I had my eyelashes done again the day earlier. My hair had decided to style itself that day by way of the hot water in the shower as I had not tied it up that time. Nevertheless, the shower style looked nice on me. I pulled up in the parking lot and parked opposite his vehicle. I waited from 1:00 p.m. to 4:05 p.m. and he never came out. I sat there still ruminating about what happened. I thought, "I told him way back in December about Esprit, that I had a daughter, and you mean to tell me he couldn't tell me he was married?" What were his intensions? I think it is called playing games. So in a sense he was a player. I'm beginning to feel like a fool. I am out here in the back of the building where he parks his truck waiting for him to get off from work so I could give him the letter (I knew he had a truck). People with the zodiac sign of Cancer have strong intuition, then you have the woman's intuition. (Also my daughter says intuition will wake up in people who have been in unfortunate circumstances). It started to get uncomfortable in the car and I started thinking about going inside through the front of the building. Sharon told me I could not come back in the building the day I was suspended. The Holy Spirit said, "Go around to the front of the building." Of course I did just that and as I passed the entrance doors a small distance, I could see Tristan there. Just so happen there was a parking spot close to the door. I quickly parked my car, got my story Monster 2004, the Change CD with "This is for the Very Best in You" and a little letter. It said, *Just you doing your job, acting respectful, having energy made me internalize the song, "This is for the Very Best in You". (#6 on the CD). I then began to exercise, felt joy, face started glowing, eyes sparkling, hair thicker, skin softer, etcetera. That is why I call you my "light." That's it."* I walked into the doors of the facility, and Tristan's face quickly dimmed and looked kind of upset when he saw me; he was talking to the facility security guard. I warmly/coldly said, "Hi"; but he did not speak. Then I had an upset look on my face. It was if we had been in a relationship. He looked hurt, and so did I. Did he actually have feelings for me? I loudly placed the 3-item package on the counter and walked away. At that time I had not seen him for days. He definitely was avoiding me, and I was taking cues from him since he was avoiding me, but longing to be with him at the same time. The Holy Spirit told me to go to the front of the building and that was where I found him. I had not seen him since we looked into each other's eyes in the cafeteria. Plato' Symposium says that we have 4 arms and 4 legs and that we split away from each other and go looking for the other half the rest of our lives. Some people say we agreed to come down from heaven and that because of whatever, we became separated here on earth and that your soulmate would not be happy until you are. Whichever may be the case, I cried on and off the rest of the evening, and I asked God why did the word soulmate, alpha male come to me if Tristan was not it? The hurt that showed on our faces still said something was there, but what? Had he cared for me also?, his feelings not being as strong because he is married, but mine because I was just in a relationship. If he listened to the words of the song, read my story and remembered my warm personality and the way I acted, he would remember that his personality and mine were both very sweet and kind.

I wrote this letter:

"Tristan,

I told you that you are my soulmate. Soulmates do not have to be married to exist. I guess you ask how I came upon the word. Well, I couldn't sleep one night thinking about you and the Holy Spirit said, "Soulmate." I then looked it up in the dictionary and going by my own personality and what I perceived to have been yours, I knew the definition described you and me.

Sincerely,

Athena

The next weekend was Esprit's prom night. I had put on my pale orange flowered dress with a tie in the back, and my brown round heeled sandals. I put on my pale orange earrings that really went great with the dress. I had my toes painted and wore a little makeup. I looked like a queen. Esprit wore a black Asian-inspired dress with a Phoenix on the front with a split on both sides. Esprit had gone on inside and I came in later. When I walked in the door, one of Esprit's teachers was standing at the entrance. We both complimented each other on our attire. She had on a black dress and I had on a coral flowered dress. I was the "Belle of the Ball" that night and Esprit was definitely the Afro-Asiatic princess. Esprit's date Ted Kerrington was tall, dark was also dressed in black and white looking dapper and handsome. He was a very mannerable and peaceful young man, a gentleman. During the prom, the principal got on the microphone and reprimanded the kids about dancing too close on the dance floor, and said the girls should have more respect for themselves than that, and the boys, too. I was sitting at the table with Mrs. Kerrington, Ted's mother, and Keedra, Ted's older sister. I got up and walked over to the dance floor, keeping watch over, and splitting up the couples who were dancing too close. The girls are so much more rambunctious than we were at that age. I think back and surmised that I never acted like that in the public, at school dances, and I never liked slow songs while growing up. In fact, I despised them. I never liked loved stories either. Soon Ted and

Esprit took pictures and Esprit and Bellows Creek took pictures. I went outside for a breather and while walking to my car, I felt lonely. Tristan did not come to the prom. I looked towards the door a few times. I was hoping he would come so the kids could see a real King. He is tall in stature and muscular. I just wanted to have one dance with him. The only song he and I would have known was "Purple Rain" by Prince and that song was played as the last song of the evening. Even though the graduation was next week, I knew we were slowly being torn apart by Time and distance. Time and distance that brought us together. I did not go to my high school prom but even after graduation, some of my classmates, I never saw again. I said to myself. "He is so strong." I told him that, and hopefully one day if and when he was very ill, or in old age, he would remember how my voice sounded and that I had told him in a letter that he was so strong. I drove to the facility and his truck was not there. I then drove to a fast food restaurant, and soon what was to be "A magical night" was over.

I continued to read my Bible and prayed. I continued to take care of my daughter as best I could even though we did not live in the same place. Saturday night I went out by myself. To my surprise, the first African American Mayor of the city, his constituents and the Move Your Boogie Body Band were there. I took a seat at one of the tables after asking politely was anyone sitting in this chair. Before the festivities began they said prayer. The lady who led the prayer said that she could feel someone was really hurting, and that she could feel it in her spirit. She prayed, "Father God I ask that you give her what she needs right now. If it is peace, let there be peace. If she needs strength, let it be strength. I knew she was talking about me. I had this feeling down in the bottom of my stomach that I had never felt before and do not ever want to feel again. I was sitting there alone dressed almost as a bride in a beige subtle sparkling corset lace top, hair pinned up with pearl earrings.

I looked as though I had lost my new husband in an unfortunate event. The people at the table knew one another from school, they said. I told them I was from Norfolk, Virginia and they asked what brought me down here. I said long story but did not go any deeper into it. When the evening was over they bid me farewell and said, "Nice meeting you." I stayed a little longer and drank my soda while sitting at the table looking at everyone dance enjoying the music. It was nice hearing some of the songs again.

Chapter 5

Existentialism

The next day I went to church. The service was uplifting and I knew that God was helping me through all of this. Jesus was guarding me with His power from going under from the frustration and abuse of my relationship, and the unrequited feelings for Tristan. When I returned home, tears were streaming down my face. As there was no one else there at home, I said, "Why God, Why God" at the top of my voice. "Why did this have to happen to me? Why do we have to be born to die and bring children to Earth, labor and possibly die trying to take care of them only to have them see us suffer and die tragic deaths?" Someone I really cared for had suffered mightily and died; it really scared me and became part of the reason why I was depressed. I thought of the movie, the Advocate and agreed at that time with what the Devil said to Reeves… that God was playing a cruel joke on Man. I said, "Why, God? Why, God? I don't understand! I don't understand!" He did not answer me right away, but a few days later.. and I do not remember what I was doing at the time, I heard the Holy Spirit say what turned out to be "Existentialism."

I had never ever heard that word before as much reading I had done over my lifetime but I kind of sounded it out and knew it had the word exist in it. I looked up the definition.

Existentialism is a philosophy that emphasizes **individual existence**, **freedom** and **choice**. It is the view that humans **define their own meaning** in life, and try to make **rational decisions** despite existing in an **irrational universe**. It focuses on the question of **human existence**.

So the way I understand, it points to freedom of choice and living life and taking responsibility for the choices you make but all the while not know whether the choices are going to end up being good or bad. Say for instance you enroll in a secretarial school, you're excited and all, you take out a loan to satisfy your tuition but then when the classes start you find there is no one there, and that you are a part of a group who has been scammed, but still have to pay back the loan you took out to attend the school. That was just an example. When the choice is not good, and it hurts emotionally, physically, socially or financially, I think it is called "carrying your cross." Reverend Funs at Abyssinia Baptist Church in Norfolk used to say at the end of each service......"Does Jesus bear the cross alone and all the world goes free? Jesus does not bear the cross alone; there is a cross for you and me."

I thought of the day Tristan put his right arm around my shoulder when we were standing at the counter and I surmised that he must have felt safe with me to do that. It was a warm, friendly gesture. No boy or man has ever done that before and it made me realize how much I missed him. I refer to myself now as "Lady in Waiting" and "That Girl" by Stevie Wonder. I decide that I am not ready for a relationship with anyone. I have mixed emotions now about being with Tristan. I am scared that it was a chance in a lifetime to be with a man who helped me feel like a "Natural Woman" and broke the chain of emotional attachment to my ex- boyfriend. He also made me feel beautiful again and I have lost 30 pounds. I did not want one night (daughter's prom); I wanted a lifetime. My mother met my father on the weekend as he participated as a choir member at my mother's church, so I guess it is befitting that I met this man, Tristan on the weekend where we worked, sitting like King and Queen at our desks. In fact, there is a movie coming out about a woman who falls in love with the office janitor. With every song that I hear and every word about caring for someone and every movie about lovebirds, I shower Tristan with kisses in the hope that I am still in his heart and soul where he can feel them, but tears streamed as I realized Tristan was as strong as my father, always at work doing his job and handling his responsibilities, taking care of his family like a man is supposed to do. The cliché' "Whose your Daddy" means that a man should not be having relations with a woman if he cannot provide for her properly like her father would. In other words, "Grown Man Business" - Brian McKnight. I said I did it correct that time, I did it almost perfectly. First he had to strike something in me or have some outstanding characteristic in order for me to even notice him. I thought of him for six months with no physical contact. Maybe if everyone could wait until they got older and started their respective careers then start looking for a mate then that time would be the right time. Tristan and I are the "Perfect Combination". It dawned on me that it was okay that we had met, and that it was on the weekend. "Saturday Love" -Cherrelle and Alexander O'Neal and "Weekend Girl" -Atlantic Star. Tristan is a real man. I am a real woman but it seemed I had arrived on the scene too late for us.

I woke at 6 p.m. and read some of my book, the Lolita Files. I then decided I would read a scripture from Day by Day by Billy Graham. The scripture said, "Commit thy way onto the Lord; trust also in Him; and He shall bring it to pass." Psalm 37:5. Since I was studying my Bible while going through the throes of losing Tristan and one day had lain prostrate on the floor I knew that this scripture was for me and that I would get my answer. The prayer for the day is "In everything I do, your will must be uppermost in my life, Lord, I, as your child, trust you to lead me."

On Monday, June 14 on TV, the Judge had a case with a couple that had been married three months, dated seven months and had a 3-month-old daughter. She said, "Love is patient and long-suffering." She asked the wife if she had experienced any of these characteristics before they got married. Judge Ephraim also said that character should be on the inside out, not from the outside in. So......Sunday morning hurriedly ushered in. I got up to go to church, but stopped at fast food and bought a sausage buiscuit and a cup of water. As I sat reading the classifieds, I got misty. There I was eating breakfast alone with Tristan probably at work, and my daughter, Esprit home with her father. I thought to myself, please let Tristan remember I first wrote him wishing for two cups of hot chocolate and some interesting conversation, but men do not think cyclical. They think linear. The last card I sent said that I wanted to get to know you so well. I really tried to get to know the guy first. In fact, you could say I thought about him for six months before I tried to make a move on him. I gave a Herculean effort, a NFL punt effort try, but it just did not work. In other words I went deep sea diving, saw the treasure but could not bring it up. He is still in love with his significant other. I had a fiancée when I was in my twenties. He broke up with me because he said he had to learn to take care of himself before he could take care of anybody else. Now 20 something years later I have met a man, who can carry my weight plus a date with, but he is married, but to my credit I can take care of myself, by myself. Just how much crueler can life be? Nevertheless, the ultimate woman is one who can take care of herself, take care of her child, and never, never never let you …. At least this is what the commercial advertising Enjolie said back in the 1970s. I remember one night I sat straight up out of sleep when I dreamed I and Tristan were about to come to blows and knew if we ever come to blows it is over. In my readings, I came upon an article in People Magazine, April, 2006, titled "What is a Soul Mate?"

A person your soul has drawn into your life to facilitate your growth.

How do you open yourself up?

Don't cling to a (certain vision). Set aside judgments and let surprises happen.

Describe the emotional experience. A soul mate makes you feel at home. I remember the letters where I was singing like a bird. There can also be a feeling of fighting an overpowering attraction. This was so true. On Sunday, I called Tristan and Vaya answered the phone. She said Tristan was on the floor. I called the front desk and asked for the second floor, and Tristan answered the phone. "Tristan, It's Athena." He either did not hear me clearly or he did not recognize my name. "You know who it is. I know you are married, but we need to talk." He answered, "No, we don't." I said, "Well, there is a reason why you wanted to chat with me, there is a reason why you just did not tell me to leave you alone until Easter, and most of all I want you to help me figure out why the Holy Spirit said soulmate and alpha male when I was thinking of you some nights." "I need you to bring that bubbly personality Sharon and the others say that you have and let's sit down and talk. I bickered, "I am not trying to be funny, but you wanted to chat with me." He then said, "I never wanted to chat with you."

I said, "Yes, you did because when I asked you did you have an e-mail or phone number I could contact you with you said, "I will have to speak to you here." I then said, "None of this would have happened if you were wearing your wedding ring. He then said, "I am not the one for you." "Well, you are leading me to him." He said, "I can't lead you to someone." I tired of trying to convince him and said "Tristan, I feel lost." He said, "Don't call me anymore. Don't contact me anymore." I tearfully said that I wouldn't. I had been looking for a picture of a black man and a black woman dressed in royal African attire both reclined shoulder to shoulder but I only found an abstract print of a woman and a man. When I saw it, I said, "That is it." It pictured what I felt we were, two of the same just one male and the other female. In the original African Heritage Study Bible after Psalms, there is information on Queen Makeda, who was the Queen of Sheba, a queen who lived in the Virgin Land (Ethiopia) who journeyed for wisdom and finds light. Makeda had the privilege of an education and had formidable knowledge of natural history, music and astronomy. A peculiar woman, she had all her life been interested in questioning the mysteries of life. She said, "Perhaps many people will say that I am inquisitive, but that is simply because they do not understand me. "I am always anxious to learn and serious-minded." Makeda then journeyed more than 1,000 miles to inquire into King Solomon's wisdom. So desperate was the queen's desire for freedom and so great was her faith upon learning the good news concerning King Solomon, she went to see him. I compared myself with Queen Makeda. I, Athena, am from the virgin state (Virginia), the mid-Atlantic southern state, had the privilege of a education, and music and I also love astronomy. For Christmas, my father bought me a telescope; I was 10 years old.

A peculiar child, I had been puzzling over UFOs, the Loch Ness Monster, Big Foot, the Kraken, ghosts, Stonehenge and the statues of Easter Island. I used to sit on the living room sofa and watch "In Search Of" by myself and watched Project Blue book on television outside on the front porch during the summer time by myself. And I traveled over 1000 miles to the Mid-South and gained King Tristan's wisdom just as Queen Makeda traveled to meet King Solomon. She could not find him at first just like I had looked for Tristan at Mt. Sinai and did not find him. I sought him just like Queen Makeda had sought King Solomon, but found him not. I will rise now and go about the city in the streets and in the broadway. I will seek him whom my soul loveth; I sought him, but I found him not. His eyes are as the eyes of doves by the rivers of water. His legs are as pillars of marble. His mouth is most sweet. Yes, he is altogether lovely. Queen Makeda said that she loved him merely on concerning him and without seeing him, and the whole story of that hath been told he is the desire of her heart. I remembered I called him my Light, and I said that I loved him merely on seeing him at work and without hearing him say a word to me. He is the desire of my heart. The Bible verse says " Trust in the Lord with all thine heart and lean not to thine own understanding. In all thy ways acknowledge Him and He shall direct thy path – Proverbs 3:5-6.

On Monday, I went over to my ex-boyfriend's house while he was at work, and the phone rang. I picked it up. It was the Navcom Company. The company wanted to send over a representative to put in some new equipment.

I made the appointment for Monday, but I knew I may or may not be there depending on whether my ex was home or not. I spent the weekend at my girlfriend's house, and came back home Monday to look at my emails. The phone rang once again. It was the same company calling to make sure it was okay for the representative to come to install the new equipment. The representative said she would just tell the rep it would be okay to come over now to install the equipment. While he was here, he and I were talking, and I shared that I no longer lived there, and that I had left my boyfriend; I explained why. I told him I had met someone and he could tell that I was getting emotional. The rep prayed over me. He then invited me to a revival at his church, and

ssed one night of the revival that week. I found that I can
ambourine, and can do intercessory prayer. I also marveled
at the stain glass window painting of a black Jesus. I have never seen
anything like that in Virginia. On the last night of the revival, the senior
Pastor thanked me for coming and commented that I had a beautiful
personality. On Wednesday, I typed some of my story and saved it in
the computer. I went to pick up some cat litter and went to the area
to Mt. Sinai to work out. There was a baseball game going on, but I
worked out anyway. Later on I drove home and looked at the sun almost
covered by clouds. It was kind of funny that today I decided to look
at a sunset longer. Alone. I probably had everybody wondering what I
was doing writing on top of my car looking at the sunset. It was 7:00
p.m., and the sun will really not set until 9:00 p.m.; it is summer. Later
I am driving down the street, thinking of Tristan. While looking at the
sunset, I surmise that he is probably watching it with his wife, checking
his oil or something. I had to talk myself into believing that I was not
out of place. That it was okay we met, but I also felt I could be highly
mistaken. This man did not ever want me, who am I fooling?

So if I did swoon over him. Today, I was supposed to send flowers,
but did not because I do not think he never really liked me in the first
place. I began to cry and was thinking about the song *The Love We Had
(Stays on My Mind) The Dells 1971.*

In 1971, I would sit on the couch in the living room and read
magazines after getting out of the second grade every day at 11:00 a.m.
As I wrote this, I sat at the window and saw a burgundy truck back up
and go the other way. I wondered if that was him and shed a tear. It
seemed we just can't get together or was he the guy I saw driving down
the street? Whoever it was he quickly backed up and went back out.
It was a long burgundy truck just like Tristan's, but Tristan is happily
married and sometimes I think he feels I am nothing more than a snake.

It turned out that it was not him quickly backing up and going back out and it is just my luck that it is not him.

The next day I awoke at 8:00 and you know it, Tristan was on my mind. At the job, my coworkers commented on what had happened but just the same my chakras opened and I gained a third eye. I felt good about what happened, but then broke down in tears. The story was the trade-off; his looking into my eyes, and I writing this story. I said this to myself with tears streaming down my face. His manly and kingly ways moved a mountain in me. It broke, tore into shreds, and severed emotionally the bond between me and my boyfriend just as it should have. These words and my tears are a testament of how I feel about Tristan, and I ask myself, "How am I ever going to forget him? I then looked up the words:

Anguish—deep sorrow.

Husband—mate of a house, male partner in a marriage

I started tearing up again, and I said to myself, "May he have a long life like my father." My father was 88 years old. I realize now I am about to start feeling the same way I did when my fiancé left me years ago. I was torn up, sank into what I know now was depression, and lost 60 pounds. I reasoned that this time I gave the best effort I could, and the words of the song called *I Try by Angela Bofield* came to my mind.

The Babylonians believed that a man should not betroth a wife lest he sees her. The (Hebrew) ceremonial civil and ceremonial law and legend explains that a person is forbidden to marry unless they see each other with their eyes. The Talmud does not say 'talk to each other, or kiss, etc.' but says a person needs to see with one's eye. This is because the eyes are the windows to the soul and 'eye contact" means your souls are communicating with each other.

Only by eye contact will you know that this person is your soulmate and only through your continual "eye contact" your souls are communicating with each other. On Friday morning, I called Alex, an elementary school teacher with Masters of Fine Arts in Creative Writing at 8:30 instead of 11 a.m. I ended up asking all kinds of questions. While trying to have an interesting conversation over the phone, we got into a little argument because I had made the statement that the slaves were docile from a passage I had seen in a Black History book.

Alex said that this statement was false, and he could not believe I was trying to put our people down. I said, "No. I am not trying to put our people down. It is just that my second grade teacher called me docile, and I saw the word a lot in the history books." He said that slaves were anything but docile. It is just what the books want people to believe. I asked him had he written anything, and found out he has printed some books. I also secured information from him about getting printed myself. He told me to buy the Writer's Digest book. The next day, I went into the store and the manager walked by and said Hello. He was tall, dark and handsome.

At the time I was not feeling really attractive, actually ashamed, but I spoke, pulled my cropped jacket together, paid for my groceries and walked out the door. I had just let my daughter off at school, and was driving down the street. I was on Winchester. The radio was not playing, and I was not thinking about anything in particular. I drive my car like a race car driver. I felt a rush. I had a rush on Friday past too. I felt happiness outside of myself, but I knew it was not me. They say that soulmates can feel the emotions of the other.

Also, I remember before I got suspended, I could feel something wrong. It was so thick; it could be cut with a knife as I walked into the facility. It wasn't just my conscious that was making me feel guilty. I talked to one of my classmates on the phone and learned that he can feel when his daughter is sick or hurt. His daughter is in Florida, and he is in Virginia. He says that when he gets this feeling all he has to do is call her mother and sure enough he would get the news. At one point his daughter had sprained her ankle and another time she was sick. This brought back a memory of when I was younger that I could feel when my great aunts and uncles were sick. I would go and tell my Mom and she would soon find out by phone after talking with my aunt that either Uncle Jean or Aunt Susie were indeed sick. I called one of the neighborhood churches and asked for an appointment with the Pastor. The day came and I drove to the church to see the Pastor. I talked with him and told him the matter. I said that I had met this guy at a facility where I worked on the weekend. I did not have to say anything else. The Spirit let him know or his years of experience told him what this conversation was actually about, and why I was there. I said I met this guy while working at the facility on the weekends. The Pastor told me simply that I had to sacrifice him for the Kingdom. While all of this was going on (the tryst about Tristan), I had sent Tristan a picture of a chest of a large sum of money in which an African man was trying to dupe me into sending him my bank account info. I wanted Tristan to show his kids what length people will go to take your money. It was Philip Nduka on the Internet. He got my email address from the website MTstars.com. He sent a sob story whereby he says a man and woman died in a plane accident and left a whole lot of money behind and he needed to send it someplace, and that All I had to do was give them my bank information. He emailed what looks like an authentic certificate with the amount of money listed.

There was a second gentleman in on it too who worked for a securities company in Africa. He had an email address and an important-sounding title. It was a money-laundering scheme that I did not fall for, but some others did. I sent Tristan this picture to protect him and his family, his little ones.

On Tuesday, I got up and went to the DMV and got a duplicate driver's license. Mine had not expired yet, but I decided to get a spare just in case. After a long wait at the DMV, I returned home. I decided to sit down and write this letter:

Tristan,

I told you, you are my soul mate. Soulmates don't have to be married to exist. I guess you ask how I came upon the word. Well, I couldn't sleep one night thinking about you, and the word soulmate popped in my head. I then looked it up in the dictionary, and going by your personality and my own personality, I knew the definition described You and I. I went to another library and checked out a book on Soulmates, which was somewhat helpful. Time passed and I had to get my TB test read. One of my coworkers out of the blue said soul mate. Mind you, I TOLD NO ONE that I was interested in you. She said your soul mate could be in a relationship when you meet him and that my whole countenance would change as it has. You know my eyes sparkled, my lips got pinker, I felt strong, etcetera. I cared about you and I still do because I feel you with me sometimes, and other times I feel empty because you are not with me. When I awake in the morning, you are the first thing on my mind. In fact, I lie there with my head turned to one side. I knew there was something wrong because I could feel it. I just did not know exactly what. It turns out you had went to Sharon. They say a soulmate makes you feel whole. You read my letters for six months. "They calmed you, didn't they? There are still some things I can't tell you because of what has happened. You put your head down and closed your eyes the last time you saw me. After you told me not to call you anymore, I promised I wouldn't. I've been trying to let you go, and it is the hardest thing I have ever had to do in my life. It seems that you are so right for me.

Athena

That Monday on Love, Inc. on UPN, they were talking about a soulmate. That weekend, Sunday, there was an article on soulmates that were married now. I read this newspaper on a Thursday.

I then happened upon this article in People Magazine on Soulmates.

All I know is this; my story has brought me to the Song of Songs in the Bible especially where she looks for him and cannot find him. She says he is altogether beautiful.

You know I had been looking for you at Mt. Sinai. After all of that hard work, I decided against sending the letter. It wasn't right. I did not want to upset him again. I also said to myself, "He never said a word to me directly. Why should I have flowers delivered? Women don't buy men flowers." I decided against it, and was glad I had not sent the flowers this morning because I felt it would hurt more than help. I felt I had made the right decision because of how I felt when I thought I saw his truck at the game. I started crying because it seems like we are never going to be together. I pulled up to the gas station to get a soda and a little girl and her father walked up to the soda section of the store. The little black girl was throwing pennies on the shelves. I firmly said, "Come and get these, and put them in your piggy bank. And when school starts again, you study hard." She said, "I will." I paid for my soda and walked out to my car. I looked to see if the little girl was looking at me, and she was. I made a gesture by touching the hood of the car, and touching my chest and mouthed: Mine. The little girl understood what I meant and I could tell she was telling her father that the car I drove was my own; thinking about the day she would be driving.

A warm, sunny day arrived and while at the park doing my ballet warmup and college dance girl routines, a man walks up and asks me how I learned to dance like that. His name was Roman. I said, "Most of it is in my heart." The young man talked with me as if he knew me all his life. He told me about his mother, grandmother, his Aunt Betty, his job and his two girlfriends. There was Emma, who is a chef and has kids. He said that it was time for her to start working, but she never started. This seemed to have upset him very much. There was also Aleisha, who lived with him. Roman said that Aleisha had no motivation, so he put her on a bus home. He seemed very upset about his situation, and I prayed over him and invited him to my church. Roman said he didn't want to drive his truck because it had a dent in the door from rushing his friend to the hospital who had been shot. I advised him to go on and drive the truck, go ahead to work until he got his finances together, until he could get another car. I told him to think about his mother's sacrifices and to help himself by going to work. I took him to the restaurant so he could get something to eat. We talked while he ate. Roman said, "I am looking for my 'soulmate." I asked him, "What do you mean by the word *soulmate?*" He said, "It is someone who will be with you through anything. I want someone who will go to the movies, dinner, parties, and will love me as much as I love her."

I was listening closely. He then said maybe the reason he has not met her yet was because he is back and forth between here and home, and that he worked at TVA. Near the end of our conversation, he told me he was going to get me something for being a friend and lending an ear. I told him that he could repay me by helping someone else one day. I dropped him off at his place, hoping Roman will pick up the reins and keep soaring.

On Wednesday night, I went to Ms. Kerrington and her twin sister's birthday celebration at the club. There was karaoke, but also spontaneity was in the air. Soon Proud Mary by Ike and Tina Turner played and some other women got the hint and joined on the stage to air-guitar, and dance like Tina and her backup dancer, but one girl stole the show.

One morning, I went to the basketball court and shot a few hoops and thought to myself, I wished Tristan could come play me. Later on that day, Esprit and I went for Chinese. We looked at the Chinese Zodiac calendar on the wall. Esprit showed me that I was a rabbit by my birth year and she pointed to the sheep as her zodiac sign. Furthermore, Esprit showed me that Bellows Creek", was an ox in the Chinese zodiac who are neither patient nor inspiring to other people. Esprit asked me how old did I think Tristan was, and I said about 30-45 years old. I told her about one of my past boyfriends, Baylor. His zodiac sign was known to be noble and chivalrous, and should marry women with the Chinese zodiac sign of rabbits. However, I never paid attention to zodiac signs. I thought a man would naturally have just as much tenacity as myself, at least anyone who I would care about. On Friday, I went to church, and there was a notebook left in which a school age girl had written notes from 2005. The year was 2006. How is this notebook in the church and sitting in my pew? It had Hebrew letters in it, just like on the soulmate page from the Talmud Kudush. On Memorial Day, I took Esprit and Ted to the mall. I walked around and visited some of the stores. I soon sat relaxed on the mall bench as if I were a Queen. I felt very comfortable because my rightful King was at work. A little girl and her mother, both dressed in cropped jeans, and flip-flops, walked through the mall. The little 4-year old lost her balloon. I also saw a young, tall man of about 25, who could've reached for it, but he didn't even try. I soon thought of Tristan, who could easily stretch his arm and grab it before it got out of his reach. I went about the next week as usual, working, writing, and taking care of Esprit. I listed to the radio. I wondered how I could just have that coffee and interesting conversation with Tristan. I kept thinking about us standing together, and looking into the others' eyes. Maybe he could be my King for a day on my birthday. I already had a pretty dress to wear on my birthday. The radio show announced that a famous boxer, the U.S. Heavyweight Champ from England was coming back to the Mid-South to visit the middle school. He was coming to congratulate the Chess team. I wanted to go, but the affair was invitation only. I decided Esprit and I would stand outside to meet the Champ and take a picture with him. The Superintendent of the City School system arrived and she was in a hurry. I told her the Champ had not arrived yet, and asked to get a picture of her with my daughter. She asked us why we were standing outside. I answered that we were not invited. "Well, you are invited now," she said with a friendly smile. Esprit and I went in and sat down at one of the tables and waited to meet the Champ, the last undisputed World Heavyweight Champion. The Champ arrived and the crowd was excited. The Heavyweight Champion of the World. His bodyguard was an even taller man. There was a banquet served and everyone got in line. The bodyguard could not join in the festivities because he had to keep things copacetic for the champ. The champ played chess with the middle school Chess team. There were speakers, including the

Superintendent who introduced Esprit as the Valedictorian of the 8th grade class with a 4.5 grade average.

The superintendent gave the Champ a plaque designed with a silhouette of the Pyramid, modeled after the Great Pyramid in Egypt, the school mascot (an eagle), a portrait of the Champ and a chess piece with the year engraved 2006. The plaque had been designed by an African American man here in the city of the blues. The Champ bought books and T-shirts for everyone, but Esprit did not want to wait until they finished the chess game to get one. I happened to look in the direction of the bodyguard, and he caught my glance, doing a fake smile. I wanted to chat with him, but could not because I wanted to be the perfect lady in front of my daughter's teachers, the principal and the superintendent, and I hoped he could understand that. I did not want to repeat what happened last time I tried to get to know someone.

The next morning I got up to try to win an all expense vacation to Disney World. I listened to the radio. I sent an e-mail explaining this is my first time listening to the radio while out of my car (Summer) and that I had been in the Mid-South for six years. I told the radio announcer the lyrics to a certain song and emailed him that I was writing a story, and the song fit my feelings about Tristan. I then asked that the dedication be from AC to TE because I felt Tristan was special. I care for Tristan and there was no dating or touching. His eyes showed me his heart. I have been thinking. To get married because you cannot keep your hands off each another is not enough reason for marriage. When you do, you will find there is nothing more than that, and that you have nothing in common or to talk about. The dreams you have will be different from your marriage partner. It is "what you want FOR…" not "FROM…" them (but I already knew this). If we have some of the same ideas, expectations, we can bring our skills and talents together to make it happen. Otherwise, the relationship will die. I knew there was something about me that kept Tristan holding on just enough. I believe he is a strong person. I know because…I was strong from what I went through, yet I still reached for love. I needed to let him go, though I was so scared to lose him forever. I never really had him at all, to be honest, but all my feelings were for him. At times, I felt like running to him because I believed I could have him, but on the other hand I didn't want to try, yet changing my mind back again. I felt I should try harder because I let my fiancé go without much of a fight. I felt like running to Tristan, hugging him, and once he held me in his arms, he would know I was his, but I didn't want to face rejection again; I feel like I may die if I had to endure that once more. I cried to see him, to be with him, to talk to him. I felt he was mine. I felt he was my life-force. His smile took away my nightmare and made me a natural woman, but I did not want to face being rejected again. I remember when I was in my 20s I had a dream that I was walking along a beach with a tall guy with broad shoulders. The guy had kind of a light voice. During that same week, I had dreamed of a little girl who I understood was to be my daughter, and we were dressed in look-a-like pink outfits. I had that dream in Virginia. When I finally arrived here to the Mid-South, Esprit was almost at the end of her third year in school. When school started in the Fall, she and I went to take pictures and she and I both had on pink skirts, and she had on a pink sweater and I a pink jacket. Looking back now I think God was telling me that I was going to meet someone significant after I had Esprit around the time we would be dressed in the same color outfit unexpectedly.

Later, I was trying to boost myself up to call him and talk to him one more time, but I just couldn't. I couldn't talk to him anymore and be rejected again! As each day passes, it feels like weeks to me. Birth is given to a new day every morning, and it dies with me no closer to the love of my life. I feel sometime I need Tristan because he is the strongest, most responsible man I ever laid eyes on besides my father. If I try to keep Tristan kind of close, I may be okay if and when my father passes away. I feel my father's time is nigh because he is almost 90 years old. Tristan stands as a strong pillar for me being so far away from all of my family and friends. I have no one else except Jesus, and my daughter. God already knew I was headed to Tennessee. Tristan was already here in place standing strong to help cement his path in the dreamer's dream. I surmised that even though we were not together, Tristan is a blessing. I felt I would be safe with Tristan, and he felt the same from me. The Internet says one feels a sense of safety with a soulmate. I felt sure about us, and that is how relationships start. One wants to be with another. I even feel calm. As I took my shower, I realized I developed feelings for a man similar to my father, who was strong and responsible. My father used to walk around the house with his cigar when we were all dressed and ready to go on a Sunday afternoon drive while saying, "I'm a man of means." I also realized that I was stronger than my mother. I had to be; I had to be as strong as my father. I went to check on Esprit, but when I checked the answering machine while the abuser was at work, I heard a message that played a gospel song." I then thought I would call Tristan. When I called the facility, Tristan answered and sounded like he was not having a good day. I said, "It's Athena." I had to say my name two times. He said, "Why are you still calling me?" Again, I was not ready for this. I thought he would be happy that I called and that it was him that had called. He said, "I don't have anything to say. Bye Bye." I accepted that he did not want to talk with me, and I did not breakdown like I thought I would. I seemed even stronger even though just last night I cried. Evidently, he must have gotten the flowers, but must have thrown away my letter. I even accidentally called the department where the Bear answered the phone. I couldn't understand why my little soul brother, Allen, missed me, yet Tristan still treated me with little patience. Even Prince, a dark-skinned man from Africa, appreciated seeing me that day. I was feeling a little guilty, so I called 411, and asked for the number of Baylor in Norfolk, Virginia. I got the number, called and it was him. I had not seen or talked to him since 1998. We talked for a long time. He said he remembered my name, but not my face. I told him he was in the Marine Reserve, he went to Norfolk State, he drove my silver Honda, and we had met at the Main Event. I told him I had been fighting in my relationship since 1991, that my daughter was going to high school next year, and that I had been in a rough relationship. He said that he was sorry all of that had happened to me. He said that he was working, and now doing photography as a hobby. In the book Finding Your Soulmate, the author says that "Like attracts Like" and that "you would meet your soulmate when both are complete." For example, a man with feminine qualities could pair with a female with male qualities. On top of that I hate being in a relationship with a man who is au contraire and says asinine things. I told Baylor I was writing a book that I can't seem to get the final answer to. He said, "No one knows the final answer to things. The questions of life are as vast as the number of people of the Earth."

I decided I would go see Pastor at church after service since he knew Hebrew, and see what light he could shine on the Talmud Kdushin 41 on Soulmates. I drove over to check on Esprit and watched the sunset while listening to the Commodores. I paid more attention to the song "This is Your Life" by the Commodores and that it was released 7 years after the "Dreamer" was assassinated. I knew that what I was writing would maybe help someone make it another day. I went on an interview, and afterwards was hungry and stopped at a fast food restaurant. I bought two chicken sandwiches, one for me and one for Esprit. On my way to the car Stevie Wonder's song That Girl played on the radio. I grabbed my baton out the car and started twirling and dancing. My pants were kind of slipping as I had lost weight, but they managed to stay up. My pants were not going to stop me from dancing. Evidently the workers on the inside had been watching because as I drove around the building one of them hollered out the drive-thru, "Thank you!" as if he understood why I was dancing. The Dream is still alive. I was dancing for Life, dancing for my mother, and for Esprit, alla us and the Dreamer being a light. The next day when I went to pick up Esprit, I found that her dad (the abuser) said she couldn't go anywhere else with me. I wondered what kind of person would try to keep a daughter away from her mother. Esprit will not grow up to be a man; she will grow up to be a woman. I went to fast food and bought a hamburger, fries, and soda for Esprit, and when I returned blew the horn so that Esprit could come and get the food. Later on when I called Esprit, I found out later that the abuser had told Esprit not to come to the car to get the food.

My question is what man in his right mind would tell his daughter not to go get food to eat that her mother bought? I spoke calmly with her that the Lord has provided us with food to eat, and that when there is food and you are hungry, you should eat.

I explained to her that her grandfather used to chop off the chicken's head and that her grandmother would prepare and cook the chicken and that is how we ate during those times. I reminded Esprit that her Grammy and Grampy on her father's side had even did what they needed to do to provide food for the family, but yet the abuser had the audacity to tell Esprit not to get the food her own mother brought her to eat. Later on that week I got up, dressed to take a keyboard typing test for the DCC position. I wore my Asian shirt, and blue cropped pants. I also had on some silver earrings. I put on my white sunglasses. While on my journey, a stoplight caught me. As I wanted for the light, I looked over and there was this guy I estimated to probably be in his 30s in a car with his school-age son, and I did the head acknowledgement. The son looked at his father, and his father smiled and did the "nod" in return. I smiled, and I mannishly turned the corner, "handling those wheels." That nonverbal communication really felt good. It was if we understood what we were doing in our separate lives, but together, putting these kids through school. I took the typing test and felt I did well on it. The test administrator said the passing score was 42 wpm. Results come in the mail in 10 days. One morning when I went to the store, I was in the beverage section, I noticed a man standing in front of the meat case on the same aisle. I could tell he was checking me out while on his cellphone. I felt a little invaded, and it still seemed he made it his business to keep looking. I went on and turned my back on him, walking away. Later on I laid on my bed eating a side salad and put a baby tomato in my mouth. It was juicy, and some of it squirted on my chest. Oh, Lord I am thinking about Tristan again. Tristan again. I said to myself, "God, when is this thing going to go away?" "When is my wanting to be with this man ever going to go away?" I got up and looked in the bathroom mirror. I showered and dressed. My makeup was doodled on, and I tried to see how I may have looked to him with my eyes. My eyes smiled, but I couldn't get my face to mirror the happiness, joy, peace, connection, affection, admiration, adoration, appreciation, and gift that I conveyed through my eyes when I looked into his, "One Moment in Time" – Whitney Houston, when our souls touched. Every once in a while the benefit of the doubt slips away when thinking about the whole calamity. I thought of how back in slavery time if Tristan had went to the Master about me, the Master would have whipped a tree on my back, and possibly had my breast cut off and I could have died from the whipping or the maiming. I surmised that it was a stupid thing for him to do just as he thought what I had done was real stupid because I got suspended. I remember when I came out of the doors and Tristan was coming in. I said, "I see you again" and he said, "I see you again." I just walked away moving swiftly like a gazelle, never looking back, never letting on. I see now that I didn't know I was beginning to care for him. I always had maintained a pleasant attitude, but I was actually crying inside. I remember that I had wrote to him that I had a lot of love to share with someone, and that I still had not found anyone special. It looks like it's still him. It looks like the soulmate is Tristan. I took a ride over to see my daughter, and Justice and Design was on and the word "Soulmate" was used. I ran to Esprit telling her the word was used again. These are reruns but not for me. This is the first time I had seen this episode. Soon we turned to the Live Show. They did a skit on prison mate.com and sure enough before the skit was over, one of actors said I met my soulmate at prison mate.com. I again ran to Esprit crying I didn't want to hear this word anymore. I remember the first response I got from Circle of Light on the Internet, they said that he was my twin flame, showing when he looked into my eyes that love does exist but at the time I felt they were mistaken, and that he was not my twin flame.

This is not the word that popped in my head when I was thinking about him. The word 'soulmate' came to my mind while I was lying in bed thinking of him and I had never heard the word before. I know Tristan is the soulmate. His responsibilities are so vast that he can't see the forest for the trees, that he is so closed up, scared to even teeter for fear of falling off. I remembered how I tried so hard to get to know him, and to do the right thing this time. I started crying again because I tried to be with him for four months, and he never really said "No" until Easter Sunday when he finally said he was in a committed relationship. I have to let him go, and face the fact today that one day he may wonder …. But it will be too late.

I went home and fell asleep, awakening at 7:00 in the morning. While driving down the street, I noticed another driver out of gas again. The second time I offered a cellphone, and the third time I met a driver out of gas I could only give $1.00. The fourth time I saw someone out of gas, a black couple was helping an elderly white man with gas from a gas can. Later that evening I drove on to where Esprit was and quickly grabbed a couple of books, and left. The ex was on the way home. The week flew by as it always seems to now, and when morning arrived, I went to church and the visiting pastor preached about soulmates. Esprit said that she thought I was going to scream while in church because the pastor had introduced soulmates, Mr. and Mrs. Balum. The pastor said you cannot have spiritual without the sexual, that they go hand in hand. When one is lacking the other becomes a dog. He went on to say that you have to spend as much time vertical as you do horizontal. I surmise that this is why the "accident" happened at the facility. I was lacking the complete spiritual side of my life as well as … and Tristan could have been lacking as well but I (Eve) bit first, and Tristan (Adam) could not, would not, did not let me win again. Adam was stronger than Eve this time and did not bite of the apple. Tristan won this go around. I'm kind of glad. I had kept saying "you are so strong" in my letters to him. I needed him to be stronger than me because my environment was making me fail. I was trying to love even though I lived in hate. I was trying to reach Heaven while I was living in Hell. After church, I went to see a movie where this man and woman end up falling in love through the mail (The Lakehouse). The woman writes letters in 2006 to him and the man writes letters from 2004 to her, but they never get to see "what was there" because of time and distance. At the end of the movie, he ends up getting hit by a bus and killed. After seeing the movie, I came home and watched TV. There was a movie on about love, unrequited love, second love, first love. It has just dawned on me that since February everything on TV is centered on love or what is thought to be love. I fell in love with Tristan IN his eyes so it was more than physical. It's as if I saw into his soul, and that is the reason for the catching of the breath, and the weakness in my knees. I ruminated over what had happened with me and Tristan for a while, and with tears in my eyes decided it was time to end the story. I want to let him know…

Tristan,

I bought hot chocolate. I wanted to be on your arm at my high school reunion. I felt that I would be so safe with you.. I felt that sure about us, and that is how all relationships start. One wanting to be with another. Just the calm and the peace you brought me….

It was evident I had developed even stronger feelings for him. My chakras had opened, my third eye opened. My ears had opened also because I could now understand the lyrics I had heard from songs countless times before. Again, the soul mate brings life to life, and this is definitely what has happened.

THE ONE

I'm the one who admired you. I'm the one who wanted hot chocolate and interesting conversation with you. I'm the one who was still thinking about you. I'm the one who gave you candy for Christmas. I'm the one who asked did you have a lot to buy for Christmas. I am the one who said "See you again." I'm the one who gave you a Valentine's card and a note from me. I'm the one whose soul you saw in the café that day. I am the one who called you asking for an email address or phone number so I could talk to you to get to know you better. I'm the one who said I wanted to know you so well.. I care, (heart) you, pray 4 U, cried 4 U, cries about US but yet is cheering for you. I'm the one who crowned you King. I am the one who adores you, misses you, and thinks about you every day. Me, I'm the one.

As I looked out the window, it started to rain. As I laid down on my comforter, thinking about Tristan, big crocodile tears silently fell out of my eyes. I prayed and asked the Lord to help me bear all of this, wiped my eyes and went into the kitchen and washed dishes. I thought of my mother of how she must have felt being in a place she didn't want to be so far from family... Living with a man who acted like he did not want to be with her.

At 11:30 p.m. I found that I again could not sleep. I put on my flowered dress that I got out of the cleaners a few days ago, and my blue tennis shoes that I danced in. I drove to fast food and ordered a burger and fries. I did not order a drink because Tahiti Punch was available at home.

The next day, I went to the mall. While in the bookstore in the children's section my eyes were drawn to a book titled <u>Mr. and Mrs. God in the Creation Kitchen.</u> I remember the day my eyes were drawn to the top of the station bulletin board in the facility and a scripture about faith was at the top. Faith is the evidence of things not seen, but hoped for i.e. I couldn't see Esprit graduating high school at the time she was 2 years old, but she is now in the 9th grade with a 4.5 average.

This is definitely something I have hoped for and to keep the faith and it would be something that I would witness. I walk by faith, not by sight.

I woke up at 5:00 in the morning. I surmised that this is what time Tristan was up but he was at home. I stayed up about an hour, drinking chocolate milk and fell back to sleep. I reawakened at 11:00, showered, and emailed Esprit to check and see if there was any black hair color in the bathroom. I decided the reddish brown was too light for me right now. I also felt maybe I would email Alex to take some photos of me to send to the magazine for the article of 2007 bachelorettes.

After speaking with Alex, I thought, "Oh My God, Help Me!" With tears rolling down my cheeks, I thought, "It does not feel right when I'm letting him go. I went to Stephenson's and picked up chocolate milk, bread, canned chicken, etc. Anthony was there on the register. He was clean shaven, bald with a small goatee. I couldn't look him in the face up close but I did look when I was coming towards the register. I saw that he had a cellphone on his pocket. I surmised he's probably married too. He probably feels sorry for me as there is no ring on my left ring finger thinking …Here is this beautiful woman going to spend Saturday evening alone.

Later on that evening while eating Shrimp Fried Rice, and watching B and B on TV in the Chinese restaurant, I pictured Tristan in a black shirt with the collar open showing just a peek of his caramel chest. I pictured sitting beside him feeding him the things he likes while lovingly looking into his eyes, getting and giving a portion of the adoration of this man. I was falling into that love trance again but shook my head out of it. I stared tearing up again and thought to myself, This doesn't feel right. I almost broke down and cried, but there were two other women waiting to be served their Chinese food so I dropped my head and forked at the food until the tears went away. I was waiting to go pick up Esprit from school. The *mail came today, and there was no reply about the reunion. I surmised that he should really try to answer because I did give him a stamped envelope with which to send a response. He never did. The finality of it lets me sleep at night but as I think about him through the day, and walk as if he is beside me, I still call on and talk with the Lord. HE is the one who has been putting me to sleep these past few days. The next day I again* awoke at 5:30 a.m. and dutifully picked up Esprit to take her to school. Esprit did not have the key with which to lock the door, so disappointingly I threw my keys up the stairs so that she could lock the door. The drive to school was fun while we listened to the TJ show and the headlines of more shootings in the Mid-South. I realized that instead of hot oil, hot grease or a gun, I chose love and it is being given back to me and then some. After dropping Esprit off to school, I stopped at the store to pick up oatmeal, milk, canned chicken, relish, and bread. I am still trying to keep off weight I had lost for my reunion that would be in a little over a month. On Saturday after watching Sparkle, I knew I shouldn't have watched it instead of going to bed, but I did see how the two main actors' could develop chemistry on the set and that part of it probably was not acting. He probably felt just as enamored of being in her presence as she did of him. How she sung with feeling and happiness is how one's mate should make them feel. Not try to stifle them or control them, but then again if you are trying to accomplish something real important, limitations are in order. I went home and thought of the flowered lapel pin that I had seen advertised that I felt would be perfect for Tristan's H.S. jacket. I would order that and put a streamer in a small box with the invitation to the reunion in it. Again, I felt maybe I shouldn't, and… First seek ye the kingdom of God and all these things will be added unto you, but at the same time I felt that God is change or that in change there is God. I just thought I would ask because Tristan was the one man covering me. He is the first real man I have ever met. I decided to send the pin with the streamer invitation. Later that night sleep eluded me, but I did manage to get four hours in, and at 6 a.m. the Lord woke me up to go pick Esprit up for school. I showered, put on make-up, my clothes, and was out the door. After dropping Esprit off to school, I finally learned the way home after getting lost a few times. It felt good coming to a place where there was no argument, no fussing, no disagreeing, just peace and quiet. A sanctuary. As I got ready to go take my pictures, I thought of Tristan, and I put my head against the corner of the closet and rested there for a few minutes. I thought to myself, "Support, pillar. This is what a soulmate is." As I stood there, I said to myself, "Tristan I need you, I need you, Tristan. If you would think back to Secret Admirer and two cups of hot chocolate. I did see your palms that are just as light as mine. I don't know why all of this happened, may be you have already served your purpose for me, but it doesn't stop the tears. Nevertheless, I still care immensely for you, and I just know if I had met you in school or in college, you would have been mine, but probably if I had known you then, I would not have seen the fine man you've turned out to be today, so it's bittersweet.

As I drove to pick up Esprit from school, I saw Kenyon coming out of the door. Kenyon is a little boy who lives in the neighborhood. I turned the car around and told him to "Come here." I said to him, "Every life has a purpose. I'm not sure how it all fits together, but for some reason, our paths have crossed." "Did you send your brother the book I gave you?" I had given Kenyon the book, MEG, about a Jurassic shark to send to his brother who was in jail. Kenyon did not say anything, so I asked, "Did you start reading it?' Kenyon still did not say anything. I told him that in the book the author described the shark's head to be as big as the front of a Ford Truck. A Ford truck then drove by, and I pointed it out. I said I really couldn't say how big the body was, but in the book the Jurassic shark had beat a T-Rex. I gave Kenyon a hug, told him that this might be the last morning that I saw him, and told him to do his best in school, and that may be one day he may be able to help his brother. When I got home, I wrote in my journal…*Tonight, I can't sleep again after seeing you. Why can't you be happy that I left that relationship. You covered your face so I couldn't see you when you drove by. I had just told my daughter not even 20 minutes earlier that you were a fine father hoping that you would give me my props in some way too.* On Monday morning, the first day of school, I think we may have passed each other on the street. One lone vehicle going one way and another lone vehicle going the other way. Later that day, a coal train held me up and then later after being slightly turned around as far as direction in my car riding with my daughter, a love train of children crossing the street held us up. Funny how the coal train comes through at 2:15 here in the Mid-South just as it does in Norfolk, Virginia. I used to have to get across the tracks before the train would come through so I wouldn't have to wait, and if I were not getting across the tracks at 2:30 and not beating the train, I was staying back after school as captain of the majorette squad. Yes, when the drum major blew his whistle, I was in the very front. That is how we ended up meeting. The expanse was in front of me, but still I marched on.

At 11:30 after watching Nightline, I showered and retired for bed. Of course, I thought of Tristan. The thought of him put me in a trance for about 10 seconds as it had many times before, but this time, no heart flutters, nothing. Time and space was increasing once again. I asked God, "Why did I meet him and then chuckled to myself that he probably asked also, Why did I meet her? On the next day after picking up Esprit from school, I went to fast food and noticed Jonathan and

Tracie, the couple downstairs. They had been having some problems, but things looked like they were going well. Jonathan said back to me what I had told them after Tristan had told me "Seek ye the Kingdom of God and all these things will be added unto you." He said that having the Lord as the head of their home resulted in a down payment on a house in Orange Mound. Orange Mound is in the process of receiving a major overhaul as it was the black "Mecca" in the 1920's. Upon retiring for bed later on that night, I knew I shouldn't have asked Tristan to be my date for my 25th reunion, especially after he told me he was in a committed relationship. I did a little shopping and talked to the owner of the store, Mr. K. He explained to me that I was on a higher frequency, and that a lot of people will not understand what I was saying, and to not waste my time trying to explain. I never asked Mr. K. about the word soulmate. Mr. K. explained to me the significance of the obelisk, and what it stood for after I asked what that was sitting on his desk. He reminded me that the Washington Monument is built very similar. I asked him about the Egyptian King and Queen in the picture on the wall, and it turned out to be Anubis and Isis. When Esprit got on the computer and pulled up the Internet we found that the tale of Anubis and Isis was a love story. I told Esprit that God is trying to show me what I had missed, that Tristan is the soulmate/twin flame, or that I was going to meet my soulmate since Tristan and I had an "eye accident". Of course, I think about him, but at the same time I realize continuing to think about him is not good for me, even though he has opened me up and I am now even writing poems, and feeling healthy and vibrant like someone deeply in love with another. As I walked from the store to my car earlier today, even though the sun is shining down on me, I am a little sad because Tristan is not in my life, and every day pulls us further apart as if it was just day 1 of our separate lives. During this season, I have witnessed three sets of twin girls. The first set, Ms. Cove and her twin sister, who live in the Winchester area, a set of twin girls in their mid-20s who lives in the Baptist Hospital and twin girls eating pizza in a restaurant. While looking at everyone inside of the restaurant being so peaceful and natural, I went into the restroom and cried. When I came out of the restroom, I had my pen and paper handy and wrote a small note to Esprit.

> *Esprit,*
>
> *I feel that if my mother was a working mom and saw people like Mr. Houston and Tristan, she would have been stern with me. I want you to be happy, so I'm going to be stern with you.*

While I sat there, lost in my thoughts, I started another letter...to Tristan.

> *Tristan,*
>
> *I'm not sure about you, but on yesterday, I felt I was losing something, and that something was you. How can you ignore what was exchanged in the café, that we were meant for each other, that we already knew each other, or in other words de ja vu, and have it end in expressions as if we have been in a war for centuries. I choose the former exchange—the one that showed me I was meant somehow to be with you, not the one that put us at odds with each other, and we've never passed a sentence between us. I care for you. I remember the smile in your eyes, your soul that made me cling to you, and my soul that needed you. I know I'm missing something fantastic with you, and as each day passes, it gets no closer, but my want and need of it grows stronger. I've never felt this way for anyone before; that's how I know this time it is real. We are older*

now and did not touch. I feel if you held me close, both our lives would change.

You'd feel like you were home in my arms.

Athena

Once I finished writing, I decided to leave. I suddenly lost my appetite, and decided to visit the Dollar store instead. While looking around, I spotted a turquoise blue dreamcatcher. It held my attention for a while. I wanted to buy it, but I was determined to stick to my budget. Later on that evening, I came home and looked up air fares on a website. They were running specials on flights, and today was the last day to book a discounted flight. I looked at the price and surmised I could beat that price. I clicked on the Airlines website, and found a flight with two seats that was only $377 with tax. I smiled to myself, but felt terrible afterwards. It sounded exciting and spontaneous, but I did not want to hurt Tristan any more than I already had. He is committed. I didn't want anyone to accidently see us. I didn't want him to lie to his loved ones to be with me. It all sounds good, but from what happened up to this point, I surely did not want all of his hard work and labor to be wasted just for one night with me. I wanted more than one night. It's all or nothing, not half. Later on that night, I happened upon Grey's Anatomy and on the episode a female patient asks the resident for a kiss since she has never been kissed, and he looks around, bends down close to her, and tells her she does not want to cheat herself. Her first kiss should be with someone she cannot get out of her head. As one may see, I am trying hard to put all of this in one neat little box and close the lid on it, but life is not like that. It cannot be contained, put in a box just like you can't control a river, i.e. "the mighty Mississippi" that helped overflow the levees in Louisiana during Hurricane Katrina.

One evening while I was alone with my thoughts, I started thinking about my father and mother's relationship. These thoughts had gone away, but they have come back. I pushed those away I thought 9 years ago. It goes to show you that Celie of the "Color Purple was correct. She said, "What you do to me already been done to yours…" This is true, it only takes time for it to come to fruition. When I went to church we had a workshop in church and I asked "Why does the man love the child, but not the mother?" and one of the men quickly answered that a child is an extension of himself and the mother is not and that is why the man will treat the child well but not the mother. Well, I think it is to each his own. My oldest brother and his wife did not act this way, and he is a Man too. I headed for the store after church and when I went inside, everyone seemed so natural with one another. I looked at other families around me and it brought tears to my eyes that it seemed they can get along so well but with my ex-boyfriend there was always turmoil. I asked myself why did I break? The answer came to me.

When someone constantly acts au contraire, says asinine things to you or about situations, always moving my personal belongings, it is like they are trying to hurt you or sabotage your efforts. Essentially they let the devil ride them for a long time against you. I awoke at 10 p.m. I slept well this time, but I have to keep telling myself, "He is married and committed." This is definitely way harder on me than on Tristan. I laid down prostrate on the floor and cried crocodile tears. On Monday, after running errands, I went to pick up Esprit from school, and there were wall to wall cars and kids. Something had happened. I went inside the school down to the senior gym as directed by security to see if Esprit was there. She was not there, so I backtracked. I found Esprit standing outside. I thought something had happened to her. When I got home,

I started shopping on the Internet, but decided to stick to my budget and not buy anything else. I moved on to looking at the latest article on Soulmates, and found through an article there were three kinds of soulmates. I said, "God, somebody made a mistake. I guess it was me." I remembered there are no mistakes as Pastors Funs, Balen, Davis, Reynolds, and Ivery had been saying, and sometimes on the radio you can hear slightly the message of Jesus in those good intentioned songs. I have heard this all my life but in more songs than others. For example, Michael Sembello's Superman from the 1983 album, Bossa Nova Hotel.

Imaginary Playmate

We are grown now and we both have families, but I fell that when you ran down the street as a boy I was with you. When you rode your bicycle I was riding with you. When you played ball, I played ball with you. I feel like I am part of you, but of course separate. I was the pretty little girl in your elementary school class that admired from afar and gave you a valentine…..

I really felt bad. I went to bed, but awoke around 4:50 a.m. My mind shifted to Mr. Wiseman who visited the facility between March and mid-April. I also remembered according to the Bible, the three Wisemen were Kings. Three Kings, Anthony, Tristan and Earl. My thoughts turned to Anthony. The last time I saw him, I was standing in front of the counter with the receptionist and he had his arm around some woman dressed in scrubs. I asked Lea was that his wife because they looked so comfortable and natural together. His arm fit right in the arch of her back, making her body rest and extend naturally from the torso up. I thought about "Goldmember" being on TV with the famous actress playing Foxy Cleopatra, and she said, "I'm a whole Lotta woman." I checked my watch and the time was 5:05 a.m. My thoughts meandered to Tristan once more. I had a lovely inner feeling that is described in the information on Soulmates/twin flames. I looked at an Essence magazine. As I finished reading the article on Love and looked at the 2006 Bachelorettes noting that a woman named Candace was the Bachelorette from the home state, Virginia, the phone rang. It was my ex. He was telling me what I already knew, that I had to pick up Esprit from school. I thought about the verse in the Imzadi poem where the author says he wants to give his soulmate the sun in the morning and the stars at night just like I had said in one of my last notes to Tristan. "Know that all of the Black Kings and Queens from the past are with you, cheering you on." A tear slid down my cheek when I asked myself, "How can another woman's husband bring some other woman joy? Is it because I actually did somehow know him before? That we had actually been together in a previous incarnation? That I actually was first and that is why I feel this deep affinity with him?" Mr. Kilimanjaro says that we are eternal. As I looked out the window, I saw Two African American females walking to school, then I saw two Latino boys following them, and tears rolled down my cheeks as I knew who I was writing this for. Soulmate. Yes. Another who is as strong as you, fending for family just like you, at the top of her game just like you without a minute to spare. Superman/Superwoman, Adam and Eve on the job, and one day I catch a glimpse of his dream, your dreams in my eyes, and our hearts beat as one, and I don't want to let go because I feel it in my soul, and hang on to what could be, what could have been.

"How can you love something you cannot see?" Pastor asked in church that Sunday. He was talking about God. I was thinking about Tristan. For 41 years I could not see him, but I always knew he was there. Someone that had my back, someone who thinks like I do, loves like I do, devoted like me, but whose companion at home is no match because there has to be one leader in every family. One member has to submit. Most of the time, it is the wife but submission does not mean take advantage of. It does not mean not doing the best you can while the other carries the load because of your crying wolf. Not getting up off your keister will cause the other to think less and less of you because they are carrying the whole load, is tired of carrying, and just for one moment the thought of us lost in the other's eyes, in each other's arms, in each other's kiss, in their safe embrace, two pillars trying to stand strong in the winds of life, wanting, needing to come together for better or worse, where even though God was manifested in each, they still felt the need to reassure each other by a touch or hug.

On awakening Saturday, I felt the Lord's wondrous power and felt awe down in my soul. I cried when I realized that the little me who cried while trying to pray is probably a 'sensitive; and that everything that I was going through at home etc., the Lord knew it, knew me and was with me while I was in it. One day the little me would realize it once I find myself, and that one day, God's will, that little me will be saying "Glory to God." God already knew my entire path even before my conception, and that every hair on my head is counted and known by Him, and if the eye is on the sparrow, I knew he watched over me.

Later on that week, I auditioned to teach ballet at Ettutu. I had to dance to classical music. I danced impromptu in my silver shoes from Payless that I bought for $7.00. I had no problem getting into the music, even though I was a plus size woman. I was still very graceful and elegant. After giving references to call about my character, they said they would call me once enrollment started to pick back up at the dance school.

On the next day, I went about my day alone. I was listening to "Let's Groove Tonight" by EWF. I felt this is what the dance girls were going to dance to at the Homecoming game, my 25th reunion. I want to twirl

at the homecoming game after I contact the band director to see what will be the featured song for the dance girls. When I went to the park I noticed a mother running with her son reaffirming to me that I can take care of my daughter by myself. I also surmised what man in his right mind would try to keep a child's mother from raising the child, not wanting the child to catch the bus with the mother, showing the child how to take a bus to the mall, ride like the mother of the Civil Rights Movements, and how the child's mother (me) rode the bus to college every morning. Also not wanting the child to answer the phone like I did at home with my parents and on the job. What man in his right mind would keep a child's mother from arming them for life?

I am convinced Tristan is my soulmate. The chemistry/electricity could not be missed. In fact, it is just like Plato's Symposium, where he says we were first 4 arms and 4 legs, and we were split apart. If you look at me and Tristan, we are both tall, have long legs. I am about half his height. I looked up the word soulmate in the Bible and the definition was not in there, but it did say that emotions are associated with the soul, so its emotion mate. Soul also means the sentient element in man, which he perceives, reflects, feels, and desires. There was also like-souled explained in the book Phil, 2:20, jointed-souled Phil 2:2, two-souled Jas 1:8, and 4:8 and feeble-souled 1 Thessalonians 5:14. Later I recapped the summer, and by summer's end and schools' start, I helped get Esprit back to school, I pointed B, Jermaine and Bree in the right direction to obtain funds for college by getting the Federal Aid Form from the public library, I talked to Jenetha and prayed over Kenyon and told him to do his best in school so that one day maybe he could help his brother and I watched and help motivate Trina Athena's girls.

I went home for the night, showered, ate, and went to bed. I awakened at 9:00 a.m., got dressed, and was ready for church. I was not sure if COGIC was the right one because they were coming out of King James and going to the NIV. I felt maybe I should go to one of the two churches on the block, both Baptist, but one a Fellowship Church. As usual, God led me to where I needed to be. I felt that Rasheeda needed me to attend this church. I felt that Jermaine needed me to make this church my home church also. It is interesting that the pastor was Mr. Carey. When Esprit was born, a woman named Ms. Carey kept her while I went to school to learn medical transcription. What Pastor Carey preached sent shivers up my arms similar to how Jackie felt when I told her something confidential while in Walmart. After church, I went to get a burger and in walked two women in their 20s. I paid attention to them interlaced with writing in my journal and saw that they reminded me of my friend, Daphine, and I. Daphine was a very dark-skinned girl, and I was caramel brown. We were like two peas in a pod. We would walk to the store during the summer time sometimes 5 times a day, and she would always buy Hot Tamales and I would buy Now or Laters. Daphine was more like a sister to me than my blood sister. The next morning I woke at 6:00, but set the timer to go off in 10 minutes so I could get a little more sleep. I could not sleep so I got up, showered and dressed, and hurried out the door. I had to drive over to pick up Esprit for school. After getting Esprit to school on time, I went to the store and purchased two apples. I went home, did some telephone work, and took a 2-hour nap before time to pick up Esprit. I decided I wanted to go to the grounds of the Pyramid. On the way we saw police cars at a residence. As we drove by, I told Esprit that I did not want to see any dead bodies, and I turned away and tried to keep my eyes on the road. I did take a peep though out of the corner of my eye, and there were six young, black males stretched out on the ground, handcuffs on with their hands behind their backs. I started talking with Esprit, and I said, "You don't have to go through that if you go to school, get good grades and try to be somebody. You will not have to worry about that at all."

Soon we found the Pyramid, and I took two pictures of the statue, Ramses the Great. Esprit took some pictures as well, and she posed for the camera. Later we got in the car, and I took Esprit to her father's house. I explained to Esprit if the pictures did not turn out right, she would have to take them again. I told Esprit that I worked hard being a majorette, trying out for the dance girl squad, ballet dancer, and now I am a health documentation specialist. I told her that if you don't work hard at anything, you will work hard on nothing. When I arrived home, I measured my oil and transmission fluids. Later I fixed my dinner and I wondered if Tristan had received the invite to the reunion because I had made certain all of the information needed was on the invitation. I figured quickly if Tristan didn't get it, well, that I would just let it go. I had bad days and good days, but it looks like it is going to be a bad day. This whole ordeal brings me back to the song Valley of the Dolls –Dionne Warwick. I am already hurting because I felt betrayed. I felt I let him in and I got too close. I had thrown caution to the wind because I felt peace and calm. I remember one morning after getting so upset with Bellows Creek, I knocked on my next door neighbor's door and when she opened flung my myself into the arms of Ms. M, the lady living there. I was clearly despondent arguing with my ex concerning something involving Esprit where he should have known better. This was in March. I surmised that I didn't want Tristan to know how I was doing and I had no one else to talk to. On that day, my ex made me feel that I should have never had Esprit. I mean he really got to me that day. He was running me crazy. I ran next door to Ms. M, my neighbor who consoled me and said there was nothing wrong with having a baby.

That is the whole thing in a nut shell. I never had any support from her so called father. On Saturday evening, I watched Carrie 2: The Rage, and then Sparkle. In Carrie 2, they talked about Romeo and Juliet. In Sparkle, it portrayed Sticks and Sparkle together on the bumpy and uncertain road of life.

The latter outcome is what I felt I wanted most with Tristan. I haven't given up yet. I still had to give Tristan the soulmate picture and book. On Saturday after working out, I wondered again how all of this happened. My father was born a little before the first World War, survived World War II, and got married. Unfortunately, his first wife passed away, but my father kept singing for the Lord on weekends, and ended up meeting my mother at a church in Southampton County and later they were married.

Monday morning after school, Esprit said she thought she had seen Felipe, the bully from her 3rd grade class, walking down the hallway and she could not get a good look to see if it was really him. On the radio show, they were talking about "The Color Purple – Alice Walker. All of the announcers seemed to miss the emotion that was being displayed when Celie's son said "Hello" after seeing his mother for the very first time. They were joking about it. He was saying Hello, and greetings to his mother in his native language, and how happy he was to finally meet her. The thing of it is that if the script had been written for him to say Hello in English, the intensity and depth of his emotions would not have been conveyed for that powerful moment. Yet, the announcers on the radio show were laughing and making silly comments about her son not knowing the English language.

Tristan,

About the invitation, *You have personal property taxes to pay, I believe. I'm sorry. I just really wanted to spend some time with you. Time looks endless, but at the same time slips away. Patience is a virtue and I never had it. Guess I need to learn it fast. Real bad.*

Athena

On Tuesday after dropping Esprit off at school, I went to take pictures in my "Queen's dress." My bronze earrings had fallen out of my ears, but I had an extra pair that I had worn during Esprit's middle school prom. I noticed I saw a lot of men and woman together, but they were not fussing, and feuding with each other. I felt bad about my mother and father's strained relationship and I started to cry, but comparing the two, I felt that Tristan was ornery, nasty, and probably not even worth being around. He was probably not what he seems, but I knew that was not true. I could tell by the way he sweetly apologized to me, his voice and his laugh. As I saw a truck pull out of the back driveway from the shop, I braced myself because I could not bear for Tristan to drive by one more time. I wanted to let him go but…

Crocodile tears streamed down my face. As I thought about Tristan and my father, each bad thought was laced with the observation of a small child hollering to eat, and a 20-year-old male sporting a fro with an older woman checking him out and this scenario of life made me feel a bit better. Later on at night, I decided to work on a math problem just for fun.

Math Problem

If gas is $2.24/gallon, your truck gets 12 m city/20 m highway, how many will you need to travel 1,000 miles. I am getting my teaching on through my story!

Looking back I had grieved my mother a year before her death, and I was grieving yet again after coming out of abuse and isolation living in the Mid-South. Tristan, on the other hand, probably was native to this place. I woke at 4:30 in the morning. I looked through my catalog and found the perfect shoes for my dress. A bronze shoe instead of a gold one to go with my dress I purchased from Nordstrom. I'll have to quickly order these for my high school reunion. I pondered over and over would Tristan even consider going to the reunion with me. I was already going to wear my Queen's dress with my bronze earrings. I knew Tristan deserved at least a small break in this window of time. We could go to the beach later on that night. If I don't ask, I will never know. If he says "no", it won't be the first time. I sometimes think I should not have sent the invitation, I thought all he could do is reject me, but it would be nice if he would give it consideration instead of silence, which does speak very loudly. He could be cordial and courteous with his reply. Something along the lines of... I am quite flattered, but I'm quite sure you will see a lot of YOUR admirers there. I'm sure you'll have fun."

I felt like ordering the book Soulmate/Twin flame, but I decided not to. What was the use? I can't have my soulmate, but I know its him. His

character is similar. He is just as noble, strong, gallant, and persevering. He is just like me. I wish I could have the day back when he was mine, and I was his through our eyes It states on the Internet that while looking INTO your soulmates eyes, you will get a big surprise. My chakras have opened, I have a "third eye" and my intuition has kicked in.

This is what meeting the soulmate will do, and that is who you are. I said a prayer. "God, since it seems I can't have my soulmate right now, help me concentrate on my job, and the two projects that I have started. These things I ask in your name. Amen." But it is, I feel, my last chance to spend just a window of time with Tristan. I feel very strongly that if he just held me close, he would agree that I am his. But if I had not tried for him, I would still be with the abuser, and that is just unacceptable. The next day, I woke up and while in the bathroom, I noticed my right eyebrow was crooked. I had made the mistake of going to a cosmetology school and got an eyebrow wax and the student did not have a very good idea of how to wax. After I got my eyebrow straightened out, I went inside the restaurant in order to stay away from my ex. I ate a side salad, and drank a Coke and some Powerade. While I was reading the newspaper, music played in the dining area. Every once in a while, a jazz track with an African beat played, and it was quite easy for me to get the rhythm, of this music, and it reminded me of the drums of the group Slave, and the song "Dreamin." What first sparked my interest in Tristan was that after I read the book Satisfy My Soul, where the author lists some of the African tribes, I wondered which tribe Tristan had descended from. The angle of his jaw speaks to the arch in my back. His broad shoulders growled strength, protection, and safety. His hands and arms holds and hug those he loves. His legs are like strong pillars that glide stealthily through time. He is a servant as well as a king, so gracious, yet very firm. This is Tristan 2006.

As I continued to sit in the restaurant and figure out what I was going to do to try out for the Sky Show, I began to write. I pondered whether I should change anything, and the answer was Yes. It's a testimony so it has to be clean, but then again I felt the book needed to stay as it was because it talks about a multitude of topics. I felt maybe I shouldn't leave it like it is, but I wondered why God sent me the word Soulmate? Or was it the Devil playing tricks? It is because he knew I was going to research it to the best of my abilities because even when my daughter Esprit was young, when our day was finished, I would say "Thank you, Jesus." I praised him and looked to him, even through burning hell-fires. I even praised him after the movie, "Unfortunate Events" because the cinematography was something I had never seen before and the period-piece costumes used in the movie were eye-catching and believable. Even with snow melting outside on the ground, I praised Jesus for the chance to see this well-made movie. I recalled how I felt after hearing Chucki's song *I Want a Mom That'll Last Forever* – Cyndi Lauper from the movie, Rugrats in Paris. I remember while at the age of 14, I was the captain of the majorette squad, and on Friday evenings when we had to do the program show and half time at the football game, my stockings had no runs because I walked to the store to buy a new pair. The ends of my baton were always clean (until I got my professional baton), my boots were always white and polished, and my pom-poms stayed full and tied tightly. If it was homecoming, I was responsible for collecting money for corsages for our uniforms. I had to walk to school to catch the band bus Friday evening to go to the game. When they lined up in the end zone, I was the first one out on the field after counting to eight. The rest of the squad followed me, but I did not have a whistle, I counted, 3,4, 5, 6, 7, 8.

The next day when Esprit got out from school, I was pointing out Esprit's top button, and how it made her look. It made the chest area of the top look unbecoming. I also made her go and get a hair barrette so she could put her hair in a high pony tail, and that on Saturdays she needed to make time to practice fixing her own hair. When Esprit brought the hair band, it was dirty. I told her she was not wearing it, and asked where the others were. I asked her if the others were dirty and scolded her about not putting them in the clothes hamper so they could be washed. When I was young I used to play with my own hair. In fact, I used to make a mistake and twist the comb up in my hair, and was very scared that I could not get it out and that my hair would need to be cut to get the comb I had twisted up in it out. Maybe I had to realize that Esprit is different, and accept that she is her own person, but I am trying to equip her to be able to take care of herself. That is what it is all about. I went to work that day and after getting off work, I went to Mt. Olive field to exercise. Later after returning home, I showered, ate, and went to sleep after reading some of the stories in a horror book. I awoke at 8:00 a.m. and again started thinking about Tristan, I thought about his broad shoulders, and they spoke to me of protection. I laid on my back and stretched, my eyes still groggy from the night's sleep. I wrote: *I feel who is supposed to be standing beside me. I know who is supposed to be holding me. God, why did I have to meet him if I can't have him in my life? Why did I start caring for him if I can't have him? He is my other half. Why?*

At 12:30 p.m. Saturday afternoon I was working on the computer. My thoughts wandered back to Tristan and I visiting VA. Maybe we could go to the beach Saturday morning. It had to be in the morning so he could see the color of the water, but I want to forget him and get on with my life. He has a family and I have to accept that. This was the reason why he can keep resisting me, but I am practically alone. Alone with my feelings, pen, and paper…

On Monday morning, I awoke, and again thought of Tristan. Since it was Monday, I was more preoccupied with work and did not think too long about him. Later, I got ready to go to the mall. While there, I sat beside a little Hispanic girl. I did not say "Hola" to her or her mother, but instead, drew a little daisy with a smiley face. The little girl happily showed her father and this caused me to get sentimental again.

Tristan,

About the soulmate thing that is going on. Everyone is finding out that his or her partner is not who they thought he/she was. I've seen women handing off the kid to the father while she stands with another man. I've seen a woman leave her husband, taking their two sons. Everyone seems to be in the wrong relationship. Seems like everyone is with their soulmate but me, the one writing about it. I was asking you what you were going through, and it was me who was going through something. I was asking you to help me without asking you to help me. I was telling you that you were strong, so you could you be strong for me, but then strong against me. I was telling you that you are like me. You don't think I wished I'd never met you? You don't think I don't feel out of place? Well, let me tell you. I'm in sync with time. The Lord knew, and he has been working on it with me for over a year now.

At 6:45 a.m., Jesus woke me up. With my first breath, my thought-sun shined on Tristan. I felt a little tired so I fell back to sleep. Almost 1 ½ hours later, I awoke again. I said to myself, "It is time for the Queen to get up." I decided to clean the bathroom up the way Ma taught me. Sweep good first, then mop. As I was sweeping, I thought about my niece, Evelyn. Her mother told me in a phone conversation that Evelyn came running in the house one Saturday morning saying that some women who passed by was looking at her as if she were crazy because she was sweeping the porch. This thought made me laugh. Evelyn is in the 4th grade. She received a NASCAR-inspired Easter basket, and plays Grand Theft Auto video games.

I awoke at 9:00 on Saturday morning. I was thinking I should take my father to my class reunion and dance with him like he tried to dance with me when I was 9 years old, but I ended up crying when my father was trying to dance with me. I got his dancing with me confused with what I saw my cousin doing while on the dance floor. Along with my parents at odds with each other all the time, it only confused me more. I just figure that if a page on Father Fracture can be on the internet explaining to us how we did not really know our fathers because they were working all of the time then Soulmate information was okay to be on there as well. Later on I went over to the field to exercise. I had a lot of energy that day. I danced to *"Painted Picture "– The* Commodores, which fitted the saga of Tristan and I perfectly.

Saturday night, I went out to a club. It was the beginning of school again, but no one asked me to dance. I noticed three 20 year old guys standing around, drinking beer. Of course, they did not ask me to dance. I was old enough to be their mother. After going home, I drank a cup of milk. I decided to write in my journal as part of my healing instead of writing a letter. I wrote: *I've been thinking about you every day for the last nine months. I never got the chance to tell you what really* *happened. I was thinking about you one night. And the word soulmate popped in my head. I thought of the words with asinine, au contraire, and tumultuous. You see I began to feel what the words meant. I was listening to the song, <u>Holding On</u> by LTD, and I figured out what was meant by the phrase where LTD sings "Who are you?" because I find that I'm asking my ex this exact question. I don't even know this man anymore. Anyways I just cannot, am not going to live with someone I don't love, and I am not in love with any longer. Within many relationships and marriages, the woman nor the man really know if the partner was the right one for them; they never truly know… they can only hope.*

When Esprit got out of school on the first day, we got lost driving trying to find my place coming from a direction I was not used to going. Esprit has been here seven years here in the city of the blues; I have been here six years, but she does not drive yet. We finally arrived at my place. As Esprit settled down with the TV, I told her to take my clothes out of the dryer. When she did not, I told her she had disobeyed me and that I was a little disappointed in her. Of course, later I felt maybe I was hasty in my judgment. She did not want to take the clothes out of the dryer because she had never been at my place before and she did not want to get something out of the dryer that did not belong to me. Bellows Creek kept her from doing things that would help her later on in life. For instance, learning the names of the streets in the city of the blues, or answering the phone so she could be kind of comfortable talking with people. In my father and mother's home I did not hesitate to answer the phone, or the door and I did end up doing it in the workplace so I was good at answering the phone and relaying messages.

After dropping Esprit off at her father's, I stopped at the mailbox and took a peak. The abuser used to fuss at me just for going to the mailbox or wanting to go to the mailbox. I enthusiastically got in my car and drove off. While I was at the light, Tristan drove by in his vehicle. I could not believe my eyes. What were the odds we would meet again on the same street? He was going from the west to the east, and I was going south to north. I did not honk or flick my lights at him. I just let him drive by. As my light turned green, I drove on across the street and thought about a period in 1999. I wouldn't/couldn't come outside after my mother had passed away. I had a dislike for sunshine at that time, but It came to me that now I was able and told Tristan that I would be shining bright as the Sun on the inside when he walked by my desk and that he not feel upset if I did not acknowledge his presence overtly because I did not want anyone to suspect something was going on between us.

I'm wondering now if this is the reason he never told me he was married. If that was the case, then it was my fault, but it does not make me miss him and long for him any less. I woke up at 4:00 a.m. and read some of the novel, <u>Evidence of Things Not Seen</u>—James Baldwin. In fact it helped me write the synopsis for my book. At 5:00, I got myself ready to pick up my daughter to drop her off at school. Esprit was silent on the ride to school as always here lately. I wished I could spend more time with Esprit. After dropping her off, I returned home. I thought about the times my ex manipulated me so that I would spill the beans about money that I had that I was trying to save. Ever since the incident in the facility I could not trust anyone. I wondered why Tristan has not answered me about the reunion yet. I wonder if he wanted to go? If he did decide to go, I wonder if I would be hurting myself more because of my strong feelings for him, knowing that he had to come back home to his family. I was grieving him now, and we never dated. Who would I be to him after spending time with him, if he decided to go back? He brought me joy, calmness, and peace. As I got ready for bed, I was thinking about my bad relationship. I prayed. I told myself I had to do what I did to get away from him, and in the process, I may have hurt someone who didn't deserve it, and my intention was not to hurt him. I care for him. He's the kind of man that any woman would want to be with if they know a good man when they see one. While crying softly to myself, I prayed he would stay that kind of man and that whatever happened between us did not make him change. I remembered seeing him in the parking lot and I smiled to myself. He couldn't tell if it was really me. I had a package to give him, but I did not turn the car around to give it to him. I could have caught him in the car if I really wanted to. I used to race the boys in the neighborhood on bicycles. When older I went to Philly with a friend; I was driving my silver 4-cylinder Honda Civic. His brother drove his 6-cylinder car very fast through the winding Philadelphia streets, and I managed to still keep up with him in my 4-cylinder, my "lawnmower."

Later that evening when I talked with Esprit on the phone, I told her that Tristan was a good father. I thought to myself, Well, maybe he is thinking to himself I am a good mother as well."

The next day I awoke at 6:45 a.m. and thought of Tristan. Anyhow, I fixed myself some oatmeal in a cup, but found out I had no sugar. As I was on my way out anyways, I went to McDonald's for some packets of sugar. I was just about to buy a breakfast sandwich, but changed my mind and ordered the oatmeal to save my waistline. I was doing really well, shaping up good and trying to eat healthier. After Esprit and I did a little window shopping, we got fast food. There were lots of families there. One 12-13-year-old curly-haired boy sat on the bench. We looked at each other and I smiled. I felt him still looking at me as if I might have something to say and I said, "I'm writing a book. It's true. Since you are in school now, do your very best." He said, "Yes, ma'am." His guardian was standing a little ways off, and she said, "Thank you." and introduced herself to me as Ms. Collins.

At the church all of the woman were excited about the upcoming Women's Retreat to be held at the center near the university. Three days in October there would be workshops, speakers, a little shopping and fellowship. I arrived that morning and I went to sign in to get my room key. I was invited to the Women's Retreat as a new member under Christian experience. The ladies behind the counter checked for my name and to my surprise it was not there. I told them that Carolyn said she would sign me up. They looked for my name again on the list and it was not there. They gave me a door key and my room number. After settling in the festivities started and there were many speakers there with interesting titles on different topics. I was interested in hearing the speaker who was featured in Chipped, Cracked and Broken. That sounded like an interesting title. The speaker talked to us and asked us all to pick up one card that best described how we felt. Some women picked up the word Chipped, a few Cracked and others the word Broken. After we were seated, she called up to the front all of the women with the word, Chipped. A few woman went to the front and she asked them why they felt that way. As it turns out even though Chipped may be the least traumatic, all three of the words had a lot of pent up emotions behind them and each woman displayed tears from old emotional wounds they have carried for years, decades or longer. The speaker then called for the women who picked the title Broken. That was the card I had picked. She asked each one of us why we picked Broken. All of the hurt I carried from my childhood came flooding back. She said, "Athena." Full of emotion, I had not paid attention that she had called my name. She said, "Athena" again. Mind you, I did not have on a name tag and I was not on the list to be present at the Women's Retreat. I immediately knew then that was the Holy Spirit talking through her to me. She asked me did I receive it. I tearfully told her Yes.

Chapter 6

Divination

I went home and took a five hour nap. I was walking to the kitchen and I heard a voice say, "Divination." I tried to undermine that it was not from the Holy Spirit and that it must be from the devil because I had read in the past that divination is of demons but I am not into astrology, crystal gazing, tarot readings, numerology etc., but as I tried to think that the word divination had come from the deceiver, my mind kept going back to the word and so I looked it up. DIVINATION---Merriam Webster Dictionary on-line gives the #2 definition as unusual insight; intuitive perception. Also perception by intuition; instinctive foresight.

I pondered more about the word divination. The definition that pertained to my situation is that it only dealt with intuitive knowledge, not crystal gazing, tarot cards, numerology, or witchcraft. Diviners were regarded as friends in the communities in Africa. That helped me feel more comfortable about the word, but lately though everything had started to take a toll on me. I am not dancing like I was. I am not as happy. I was more subdued. I am eating more now, and gaining some of the weight back that I had lost. I shook my head. "How can this all be?" I remembered the rejection I felt at my first high school dance. When the slow jam played everyone had a partner, but me. It was like I was "Ugly Betty," but this was how I felt and all of this kind of started this whole story. Fear of rejection, experience of inadequacy, feeling of abnormality, and loneliness. Reading James Baldwin's Evidence of Things Not Seen, I came upon the Mantra—The Spirit of the South is the Spirit of America. After reading this now, I wished I had not mailed the invitation

I forgot to write down who the invitation was supposed to go to. Hopefully, the person in the mailroom would remember the notes and things from last year and place it in his box. After tears ran down my face as I surmised that I probably hurt him again, that this was unwarranted, that he thought there was something seriously wrong with me, I still hoped and prayed that the invitation got to the right place. Everything was always wrong about this relationship, and I had told that Pastor I was willing to give him up for Christ, and to work on building His kingdom. The relationship just didn't seem meant to be. There was a stumbling block in place with every step forward I took. One step forward and thirty-five steps back. I was running away, pulling away, trying always through this story and in real life. For the past two weeks I hadn't been getting a lot of sleep even with no one to bother me. Oh, God. What happened to the world we used to play in? What happened to the world that used to smile with the sunshine of a new day? Now, right is wrong, wrong is right, no one gives the benefit of the doubt. So much to do all the time that we have no time to look at things concretely. I hoped that if Tristan looked at everything with the good intentions (secret admirer), two cups of hot chocolate, he would see that it was the most innocent of exchanges, but how could a pit of Hell be conjured from Sweet Honesty? Earth is Hell. Pastor said for me to sacrifice by giving him up, but it seemed I never had him—ever since he walked out of the café six months ago.

Aint' No Mountain High Enough- Tammy Terrell and Marvin Gaye. If I was in space, I would fight the Alien. If I was in a jungle, I would fight the anaconda or a lion. I just hoped that he did forgive me. Jesus dried my tears, and I thought about what I had said. Doggone it! Those are darn-burn-it near vows! I then said, "But I need to be dying for you, Lord." The thought of helping younger kids crossed my mind again.

I felt I would like to do what Jackson did with "I AM SOMEBODY!"

I NEVER...

I never stood next to Jesse even though I chanted his words and ideas.

I never stood next to Martin ....even though at the age of 6 I looked reverently at a Life magazine picture where a horse led his coffin. I never stood next to Malcolm even though his story is paramount in Black History as well, and women used to faint over Marvin and Teddy, but ...... "Starlight, star bright. First star I see tonight. I wish I may, I wish I might, have the wish I wish tonight."

The next day when I returned from the interview with Enterpro, I finally got my computer and cords out of the car. When I put the last of the computer down on the table, my eye was drawn to a gold book that had a picture of an open Bible on it. The name of the book was What Does the Bible Teach? In there I found a chapter called How Demons Mislead. I read it. One type of bait used by the demon is divination. What is divination? It is an attempt to find out the future or about something unknown. Some forms of divination are astrology, tarot cards, crystal gazing, or palmistry. I do not and have never delved into those kinds of things. My divination was intuitive perception. People under the Zodiac sign of Cancer are naturally intuitive and then there is women's intuition, and on top of that the intuitive perception. Maybe this is what my junior high English Composition teacher, Mr. Cohen, meant when he said that one day there would not be any money. I guess while teaching probably 30 years and seeing all of the kids coming through someone with an intuitive mind would probably speculate something like that. Esprit told me that intuition becomes stronger when you have been under stress or pressure. I have tried to tell myself there is no such thing as a soul mate. It was only just if a man and a woman lock eyes, and the chemistry is there, then this is what it is plain and simple. Soulmate, trollmate, playmate, checkmate. I cried when it seemed to me that the devil was using me to try to hurt Tristan even though I really cared for him. I got furious with the enemy and said, "I rebuke thee Satan in the name of Jesus." I surmised that he was already at Esprit from the way she was acting. Acts 16-18 mentions a domain of divination that enabled a girl to practice the art of prediction, but she lost this ability when the demon was cast out of her. Again, I have divination that involves intuitive perception. I use deductive reasoning a lot in dealing with people, but if I had prayed to the Lord about sending the invitation to the high school reunion, maybe I wouldn't have sent it. I went about my day as usual, went to the store to get some milk. I could not see the expiration date. The milk ended up being bad, so I went back in and got another gallon and a small chocolate milk. I also looked at the magazines. Everyone was going about his or her day in the usual way. I am the story teller from all of my experiences, and every time I write something I am paying homage to my Queen and I wonder if anything I have written is going to ever be printed. I have to keep praying, keep going and leave it in the Lord's hands which is so hard for me to do. I am an alpha female, and I am used to pushing everything. It is as though if I don't make it happen, nothing gets done.

Chapter 7

Ecclesiates

I was quietly washing the few dishes that I had used for lunch. I was just about done when I heard the Holy Spirit say the sound ECCL. I felt that was a little strange because everything else that I had heard was a full word, but I Got it! I said aloud, Ecclesiastes! (The significance for me of the Holy Spirit just saying the sound E-C-C-L and not the whole word is that in medical transcription, my field of expertise, the medical language specialist (transcriptionist) uses the sounds of letters to figure out the names of medications, tests and medical conditions to develop complete healthcare records for patients. For instance, aphasia and aphagia. Aphasia, the first term of the two deals with language--speaking, listening, reading and writing and the latter, aphagia, is the inability or refusal to swallow. Also there is Zanaflex and Xanax medications. The first letter in Xanax is X but it sounds like a Z and the first letter in Zanaflex is Z. Even though the sound of the first letter in Xalatan sounds like a Z,it is spelled with an X. In other instances the sound ph can really be an f and vice versa, and the sound of the letter y may sometimes be the letter i and vice versa ….i-s, u-s and a-s can be at the ends of medical words as well and are sound-alikes. The Holy Spirit used the sound ECCL the way I do in order to produce an accurate healthcare record involving tests, diseases, disorders, medications and procedures. The health documentation specialist has to figure out, then verify the correct spelling of the dictated word in the context of each individual patient's case.

A Time for Everything

There is a time for everything. And a season for every activity under the heavens:

"A time to be born and a time to die, a time to plant and a time to uproot, a time to kill and a time to heal, a time to tear down and a time to build, a time to weep and a time to laugh, a time to mourn and a time to dance, a time to scatter stones and a time to gather them, <u>a time to embrace and a time to refrain from embracing</u>, a time to search and a time to give up, a time to keep and a time to throw away, a time to tear and a time to mend, a time to be silent and a time to speak, a time to love and a time to hate, a time for war and a time for peace."

Ecclesiastes 3:1-8

Have respect for God and OBEY his commandments. That's what EVERY ONE should do.

P.S. While reading my Bible I found that it Is not good works that save us which I had believed ever since the age of 9 from a song sung at my grandmother's funeral. It is by grace that we are saved through faith-and this is not from ourselves, it is the Gift of God. Ephesians 2:8

Infinite

Bibliography

The Bible

For God hath not given us the Spirit of fear; but of power and of love, and of sound mind.
2 Timothy 1:7 KJV

Trust in the Lord with all thine heart and lean not unto thine own understanding. In all thy ways acknowledge him and he will direct thy path.
Proverbs 3:5-6 KJV

Commit thy way unto the Lord. Trust also in Him; and he shall bring it to pass.
Psalm 37:5 KJV

Used by the Holy Spirit

Of course, The Bible.

Purchased pop-up "The Jungle Book" at book fair in elementary School - Virginia

Virginian Pilot Classroom Spelling Bee Champion 5th grade, 2nd runner up in elementary school Spelling Bee - Virginia

Started medical transcription in 1994 involving medical language--root words, combining forms etcetera, and letter sounds further explained in Chapter 7.

The Internet (Google) Merriam-Webster Dictionary

Existentialism - Popularity Top 10% of Words

> : a chiefly 20th century philosophical movement embracing diverse doctrines but centering on analysis of individual existence in an unfathomable universe and the plight of the individual who must assume ultimate responsibility for acts of free will without any certain knowledge of what is right or wrong or good or bad

BOOKS

Evidence of Things Not Seen, James Baldwin 1985
Henry Holt and Company

Mr. and Mrs. God In the Creation Kitchen, Nancy Wood 2006
Candlewick Press, U.S.

But the helper, the Holy Spirit, whom the Father will send in My name, He will teach you all things, and bring to your remembrance all that I said to you (John 14:26).

Jesus said to them (apostles) When He, the Spirit of Truth, comes, He will guide you into all the truth, for He will not speak on His own initiative, but whatever He hears, He will speak; and He will disclose to you what is to come. He will glorify Me, for He will take of Mine, and will disclose it to you (John 16:13-14).

Does God Speak Today Apart from the Bible? R. Fowler White

Movies

Brewster, C. (2005) *Hustle & Flow*. USA: Crunk Pictures, Homegrown Pictures, MTV Films, and New Deal Productions

Bergqvist, S., Demeyer, P. (2000) *Rugrats in Paris: The Movie*. USA: Paramount Pictures and Nickelodeon Studios.

Siberling, B. (2004) *A Series of Unfortunate Events*. USA: Paramount Pictures, Dreamworks Pictures, and Nickelodeon Pictures.

Argesti, A. (2006) *The Lake House*. USA: Warner Bros, Village Roadshow Pictures, and Vertigo Entertainment.

Shea, K., King, S. (1999) *The Rage: Carrie 2*. USA: Red Bank Films and United Artists.

O'Steen, Sam. Sparkle (1976). Warner Bros, Warner Home Video.

The Color Purple
Spielberg, Steven
Warner Bros., Amblin Entertainment 1985

The Passion of the Christ
Gibson, Mel
Icon Production 2004

TV

Enjolie Perfume commercial 1970's

Magazines

"What is a Soulmate" *People* Magazine 2006

Music

Sembello, Michael "Superman"
Bossa Nova Hotel
Warner Bros. 1983 Album

Painted Picture, The Commodores
Motown 1982 Single 7" Vinyl

Houston, Whitney "One Moment in Time"
By Hammond, Albert, Bettis, John
1988 Summer Olympics Album
Arista 1988 Audio cassette

McKnight, Brian "Grown Man Business"
By Marcus Miller
Brian McKnight Gemini
Motown 2005 CD

LTD "Holding On"
By LTD Togetherness
A&M 1978 Album

** Dells, The "The Love We Had Stays on My Mind"
By Junior, Marvin Freedom Means
Chess 1971 Album

Kelly, R. "U Saved Me"
Happy People/U Saved Me
Jive 2004 CD

Commodores, The "This is Your Life"
Richie, Lionel Caught in the Act
Motown 1975 Album

Earth, Wind and Fire "Let's Groove Tonight"
White, Maurice, Vaughn Wayne Raise
Sony Music 1981 Album

Wonder, Stevie "That Girl'
A Time to Love
Tamla 2005 Album

Cherrelle and Alexander O'Neal "Saturday Love"
Jam, Jimmy and Lewis, Terry High Priority
Tabu 1985 Album

SOS Band "Weekend Girl
Jam, Jimmy, and Lewis, Terry Just the Way You Like It
Tabu 1984 Album

*** Slave " Dreamin'"
Adams, Mark Antone/Arrington,Steve/ Jones, Starleana/Miller, Floyd/
Turner, Ray/ Washington, Steve Stone Jam
Cotillion Records 1980 Album

Ingram, James "You Make Me Feel Like a Natural Man"
Goffin, Gerry, King, Carole and Wexler, Jerry It's Real
Quest/Warner Bros 1989 Cassette

Gaye, Marvin and Terrell, Tammy "Ain't No Mountain High Enough"
Ashford, Nickolas and Simpson, Valerie
Gaye, Marvin and Terrell, Tammy United
Motown 1967 Album

Change "This is for the Very Best in You"
Petrus, Jacques Fred and Malavsi, Maro
Change Sharing Your Love
Atlantic 1981 Album

Prince "Purple Rain"
Prince, The Revolution
Warner Bros. 1984 Album

*** Dells, The "I Touched a Dream"
Record, Eugene
Fox and Virgin Records 1980 Album

Aguilera, Christina "Ain't No Other Man"
Back to Basics
Sony 2006 CD

Warwick, Dionne "Valley of the Dolls"
Written by Previn, Andre and Dory
Warwick, Dionne
Produced by Bacharach, Burt and David, Hal
Scepter 3/23/1968 (I am writing this in March 2016) Album

Hamilton, Anthony "Coming From Where I'm From"
Batson, Mark and Hamilton, Anthony Coming From Where I'm From
So So Def 2013 CD

Bofill, Angela "I Try"
Gray, Macy/Lim, Jinsoo/Ruzamn, Jeremy, Wilder, Bofill, Angela
Bofill, Angela Angel of the Night
GRP Records 1979 Album

Lauper, Cyndi "I Want A Mom Who Will Last Forever"
Epic 2000

Guy "Her"
Davidson, Hall, Riley
The Future
Uptown/MCA 1991 Cassette

You Devaughn, Raheem The Love Experience CD 2005

About the Author

On weekdays, Athena Coleman works as a health documentation specialist in the Mid-South. She can be found catching up on the reading of two books in the same time period, one she reads at home while penning short stories of her own, and the other during break at work. Athena feels that her early love for books and being the 2nd runner up in her elementary school spelling bee has helped her tremendously with writing stories. She is extremely excited about this work of nonfiction which she says fits under the genre of "Amazing Stories" but is a memoir. She says, "Life may not give you everything you want, but you may get some surprises.

Printed in the USA
CPSIA information can be obtained
at www.ICGtesting.com
LVHW091718260224
772870LV00033B/452